– A PRACTITIONER GUIDE

Other publications by Van Haren Publishing

Van Haren Publishing (VHP) specializes in titles on Best Practices, methods and standards within four domains:
- IT management
- Architecture (Enterprise and IT)
- Business management and
- Project management

VHP is also publisher on behalf of leading companies and institutions:
The Open Group, IPMA-NL, PMI-NL, CA, Getronics, Quint, ITSqc, LLC, The Sox Institute and ASL BiSL Foundation

Topics are (per domain):

IT (Service) Management / IT Governance	Architecture (Enterprise and IT)	Project/Programme/ Risk Management
ASL	Archimate®	A4-Projectmanagement
BiSL	GEA®	ICB / NCB
CATS	TOGAF™	MINCE®
CMMI		M_o_R®
CobiT	**Business Management**	MSP™
ISO 17799	EFQM	*PMBOK® Guide*
ISO 27001	ISA-95	PRINCE2™
ISO 27002	ISO 9000	
ISO/IEC 20000	ISO 9001:2000	
ISPL	SixSigma	
IT Service CMM	SOX	
ITIL® V2	SqEME®	
ITIL® V3	eSCM	
ITSM		
MOF		
MSF		
ABC of ICT		

For the latest information on VHP publications, visit our website: www.vanharen.net.

The Service Catalog

A Practitioner Guide

Van Haren
PUBLISHING

Colophon

Title:	The Service Catalog - A Practitioner Guide
Series:	Best Practice
Author:	Mark O'Loughlin (IT Alliance Group)
Editors:	Jan van Bon (Inform-IT, managing editor) Mike Pieper (Inform-IT, editor) Annelies van der Veen (Inform-IT, editor)
Publisher:	Van Haren Publishing, Zaltbommel, www.vanharen.net
ISBN:	978 90 8753 571 1
Copyright:	© Van Haren Publishing 2009
Edition:	First edition, first impression, February 2010
Design & layout	CO2 Premedia bv, Amersfoort-NL

For any further enquiries about Van Haren Publishing, please send an e-mail to:
info@vanharen.net

Foreword

I was pleased to be asked to provide a foreword to this book. The book aims to provide an understanding on the types of services that can (or often, should) exist and how they all fit together from the customer, business and IT perspective. The book is admirably vendor and framework neutral and references ITIL, MOF, ISO/IEC 20000-1:2005 and USMBOK throughout to put services and the service catalog in the context of more than one framework, hopefully providing as broad a scope as possible.

The service catalog, as with the service portfolio concept, has come to mean many things, the content of them largely being determined by the perspective of the individual or organization offering opinion. Thus the organization purchasing a catalog product and indeed the unfortunate user of that product might well find that their own expectations are somewhat different as to the capabilities of the product.

Putting aside the vagaries of what a "product" should actually provide, the purpose of a catalog (or portfolio) is often not fully determined prior to acquiring software support. Further it is common to discover that products have been purchased for the IT domain assuming use by the business without ever consulting the business about content.

For example, the whole issue of what could/should be in a catalog is a strategic study and involves governance, management and security issues. Is the intention to have a catalog of lines of business? If so, what are the risks to the business, has anyone considered identity and access rights, segregation of duty issues and the possibility of fraud or embezzlement?

What about including applications? Which ones, and again, just what are the implications for the business if users can obtain applications in the catalog? What about "IT services" which are often incorrectly defined as being business services (for example on-boarding new employees). Depending on who you work for and who pays the bills, the "IT service" might well be IT being told to get fifty people ready for work on Monday morning. IT may wish to push that work back to a super-user working in the business area, but not everyone will see that as being an IT service then.

What about password resetting? IT service or just something that would be expected by today's "IT savvy" business customer? Well, here again it depends on who is paying the bills and what the budget holder is expecting for the money. It also of course has identity and access considerations.

This foreword is not intended to rewrite Mark's book; it is just to preface your expectations about the service catalog, its (possible) place in society and the implications -and vagaries-of its use. As with all innovations, frameworks, initiatives and projects, there are benefits and risks. As with all of these things, the complexities and the cause and effect of situations are often overlooked until later, when as usual, something has happened that was not foreseen in the rush to embrace the latest and greatest.

This is a good book. Take the time to understand the issues and if you do decide to start collecting for your catalog you will have a better chance of doing it well.

Brian Johnson
Hon. Lifetime vice president itSMF and author/contributor to ITIL and other life changing good practices.

Acknowledgements

We like to thank the team of experts involved in the production of this publication.

First of all we like to thank **author** Mark O'Loughlin for gathering best practice on the service catalog, using his own extensive knowledge and experience, existing literature and information from peers. We sincerely thank Mark for his enthusiasm and persistence, and his willingness to listen to the reviewers and seriously consider their issues. This has enabled us to develop a true *best practice* on the service catalog.

Review team
We also wish to thank the international team of experts who have reviewed the manuscript. They provided the author and editors with encouragement, criticism and useful ideas, to ensure that the book reflects the very best practice. Their expert help has been invaluable.

We thank Aad Brinkman (Apreton, NL)), Janaki Chakravarthy (Infosys, India), Peter van Gijn (Logica, NL), Linh Ho (Compuware, USA), Kevin Holland (NHS, UK), Steven J. Loftness (Sundoya, USA) for their contribution to the "backbone" of the book, the table of contents.

We thank the following experts for reviewing the completed manuscript:
- Hans Bestebreurtje, HP, Netherlands
- Bart van Brabant, Eneco, Belgium
- Federico Corradi, Cogitek, Italy
- Rosario Fondacaro, Quint Wellington Redwood, Italy
- Peter van Gijn, Logica, Netherlands
- Kevin Holland, National Health Service, United Kingdom
- Gareth Johnston, ParryMcGill LLC, Switzerland
- Steve Loftness, Sundoya, USA
- Jeb McIntyre, AIT Partners, USA
- Herve Meslin, ICT Services Department of Immigration and Citizenship, Australia
- Vernon Palango, InteQ Corporation, USA
- Neil Pinkerton, Laughingtree, Australia
- Claudio Restaino, BITIL, Italy
- Rui Soares, GFI, Portugal

Together, they produced approximately 750 issues, which were all taken in account by the editors and author Mark O'Loughlin, improving the manuscript to align with all the expert opinions on what this book should contain. With a final sign-off, all reviewers confirmed that the issues were processed to their satisfaction.

On the author

Mark O'Loughlin (IT Alliance Group) is an experienced consultant and specialist in IT service management (ITSM) frameworks, IT governance and various standards. Mark played a pivotal role in the first ISO/IEC 20000 certification to be awarded to an organization in Ireland as an architect, process manager and systems integration expert. He has achieved the ITIL Expert, Managers, Foundation and various practitioner certifications, is actively involved in his local itSMF chapter and is the editor of the chapter's newsletter. Mark also writes about service management frameworks such as ITIL, MOF, COBIT, ISO-20000 and FITS and on the topic of ITSM. He authored a "best practice" guidance about the service catalog and service portfolio which has been published in *IT Service Management, Global Best Practices - Part One*.

Contents   finished 4/26/2015

x

Introduction

Organizations today are struggling to identify what services they provide (or rely on) to enable business objectives and outcomes. Organizations have found it difficult to understand the different types of services that exist and fail to record this information in a useful and meaningful way.

This book aims to provide practical advice and information that will help organizations to understand how to design and develop a service catalog and to understand the role that the service catalog performs within the service portfolio. To this end, the book will explore the fundamentals of what constitutes a service in the hope of addressing the age old question "what is a service"?

The information contained in this book is intended for those who are about to begin their journey of designing and developing services and service catalogs or for those who have begun but would like assurances that they are on the right track. For those that are mature in their processes they may like to use this as a comparison for their implementation of services and service catalogs. Either way, read on.

Focus will be placed on arming the reader with information and knowledge that will help with:
- understanding what a service catalog is and what it is not
- understanding what the service portfolio is
- providing enough understanding to aid in the basic design of each element of the service catalog
- describing the different types of services within an organization
- showing how all the pieces of the puzzle fit together via the service portfolio pyramid

It is also evident that the service catalog requires ongoing investment, development, ownership and management backing to ensure that it:
- is valid
- is kept up to date
- is scalable
- remains relevant
- provides benefit to users
- adapts to changes in user and business needs and requirements
- is fit for purpose and fit for use
- provides value to the organization and customers
- facilitates doing business in a cost effective manner
- aids organizations in reaching new markets and new customers
- provides value for money and can demonstrate not only Return on Investment (ROI) but also Value on Investment (VOI)

Due to the nature of what is expected and required of certain elements of the service catalog, they may require specialist application software to be fully deployed and utilized. Such software can be custom-made or off-the-shelf. However the focus of this book will be geared towards providing guidance aimed at how to develop a structure for the service catalog and its various elements, independent of the platforms or applications that are available. This is pivotal when looking to setup and implement a service catalog.

It should be noted that from the start this book references a number of different service types. To just keep the discussion limited to IT services is inadequate. If IT is to earn its place in the organization and be recognized as a key business enabler IT needs to stop talking just about IT services and instead talk about the value that is provided to the business by enabling business and customer services that facilitate outcomes that the organization wants to achieve. This is a fundamental change in thinking and practice but in order for organizations to make the change they need to have relevant information that helps them understand the concepts and turn them into reality.

Some of the concepts and guidance provided in this book will be different to the current thinking and understanding of some readers. This book provides the opportunity to challenge existing thinking and presents the opportunity to embrace an explorative understanding of the realm of the service catalog.

In summary, this book can provide a catalyst to achieve a harmonized understanding of services and how they fit into the world of organizations, businesses, suppliers, vendors, and, last but not least, the users and customers.

How to use this book

This book is part of a series of practitioner books that deal with the core elements of IT service management (ITSM). Appendix A provides the basic concepts for IT service management, and is the common philosophy for all books in this series. It is important that anyone - who is not fully aware of the differences between processes and functions - reads this Appendix to avoid conceptual errors in the embedding of service catalog management in their organization.

ITIL and IT service management are most often related to process-based approaches, and service catalog management can follow that approach. Although service catalog management has its own distinct process in ITIL, traditionally it may have been placed as an element of what is often perceived as "the service level management process", which actually is a group of processes:
- contracting and implementing new or adapted IT services
- reporting and evaluating contracted IT services
- managing the service catalog

In this context, service catalog management delivers the foundation that is required for the other two main elements of service level management, as well as for the daily interaction between the provider and the users of the IT services.

Structure of the book

This book is structured into seven chapters.

The first two chapters offer the basics for the book. Chapter 1 describes the context of the service catalog and chapter 2 explains the basic principles followed in this book, and the terms used.

Chapter 3 focuses on the question "what is a service catalog?" and discusses the various forms of the service catalog.

Chapter 4 and 5 focus on the "how" question: how to create a service catalog and how to develop the different service catalog types.

Once you have created the service catalog, it has to be managed. Chapter 6 shows what is required to manage the service catalog.

Chapter 7 looks at technology considerations for service catalog.

The author closes the book with a final thought.

The remaining chapters are appendices and contain useful information:
- Appendix A provides the basic concepts for IT service management, and is the common philosophy for all books in the Best Practice series.
- Appendix B provides a simple, everyday example of where customer, business and IT services can be found.
- Appendix C lists the acronyms used.
- Appendix D provides details about the frameworks and standards referenced throughout this book.
- Appendix E provides an example of the content that should exist within a service level agreement.

1   Setting the scene

This chapter introduces the what, why and how of the service catalog by describing its context. It ends with an overview of qualifications and standards.

1.1   ITIL and the service catalog

Many people had their first introduction to the actual concept of a service catalog with ITIL. The glossary in the Service Delivery book, from the previous version of ITIL, defined a service catalog as a "written statement of IT services, default levels and options". This definition is limiting and does not represent the true value that can and should be provided by a service catalog. The Service Delivery book also provided a diagram of what ITIL perceived as being an actual service catalog which is contained within "Annex 4B of Chapter 4" (see figure 1.1).

ITIL describes itself as a source of *good practice*. In 2007 ITIL version 3 was made publically available. ITIL provides guidance on *what* should be aimed for but does not necessarily provide the information and detail on *how to* achieve the stated objectives. Remember though, that ITIL is a framework of good practice and therefore should not necessarily be expected to provide specific *how-to* levels of detail. That is where this book comes into use, at least in regards to the service catalog, and to a lesser degree, the service portfolio, by providing information that will help the organizations to:
1. fully understand the full concept of the service catalog
2. fully understand the scope of the service catalog
3. understand how to build a service catalog
4. understand the true value that a service catalog can deliver to an organization

Further, ITIL continually refers to IT services within the service lifecycle when in fact there are a number of different service types that exist. These service types will be identified in section 2.4.1 and discussed in detail throughout this book.

Over the years technology has advanced at a colossal pace and the way organizations do business with and interact with customers has radically changed. Software vendors have entered the realm of the service catalog space, in some cases, bringing with them their own, usually disparate interpretations of the concepts, scope, benefits, and building instructions regarding service catalogs. Products emerged that claimed to provide the ability for an organization to create service catalogs to varying degrees. Some were, and still are, capable of providing a solid foundation for building a service catalog. Some still have a long way to go before they can realistically offer something of value. More and more service management systems are now offering a service catalog as part of their core offering and some offer a service catalog as a module that can be licensed. Others may offer the ability to interface with different service catalogs and other service management modules, for example the Configuration Management Database (CMDB) or Configuration Management System (CMS).

Annex 4B from the Service Delivery book is shown in table 1.1.

Annex 4B Example of a simple Catalogue										
Service	Customer	Accounts	Sales	Marketing	Legal	Production	Retail	Warehouse	Transport	Design
Payroll System		✔			✔					
Accounts Sysytem		✔	✔	✔	✔		✔			
Invoicing		✔	✔				✔			
Coustomer D/Base		✔	✔	✔	✔		✔	✔	✔	
Sales D/Base		✔	✔	✔			✔			
Stock Control						✔		✔	✔	
Legal System					✔					
Factory Production						✔		✔		✔
Suppliers D/Base		✔	✔	✔	✔	✔	✔	✔	✔	
Ordering		✔	✔			✔	✔	✔	✔	
Logistics						✔		✔	✔	
Postal Addresses		✔	✔	✔	✔	✔	✔	✔	✔	✔
CAD/CAM						✔				✔
Intranet		✔	✔	✔	✔	✔	✔	✔	✔	✔
Internet		✔	✔	✔	✔					
Routemaster		✔						✔	✔	
Office Suite		✔	✔	✔	✔	✔	✔	✔	✔	✔
E-mail		✔	✔	✔	✔	✔	✔	✔	✔	✔

Table 1.1 Example of a simple service catalog (Source: Service Delivery Book ITIL version 2, OGC)

The current version of ITIL has certainly improved on this and now has a specific chapter on Service Catalog Management in the Service Design book. Table 1.2 depicts how ITIL now represents the service catalog.

Service Name	Service Description	Service type	Supporting services	Business Owner(s)	Business Unit(s)	Service Manager(s)	Business Impact	Business Priority	SLA	Service Hours	Business Contacts	Escalation Contacts	Service Reports	Service Reviews	Security Rating
Service 1															
Service 2															
Service 3															
Service 4															

Table 1.2 Example of a simple service catalog (Source: Service Design Book ITIL version 3, OGC)

1.2   Why a service catalog

The failure of IT to show to the organization the value for money that IT provides and its role in the achievement of business outcomes may leave IT vulnerable in the sense that it is seen as not being as strategically important to the organization as other business processes and functions. If IT fails to provide quality services that are required by the organization, or even fails to cope with changing demands, once again IT may be viewed as a less important strategic asset within the organization. This could lead to the possibility of areas within IT, or IT itself, being downsized · or even outsourced.

For IT to be fully successful, IT needs to be strategically aligned to the business and positioned as a key enabler in achieving successful outcomes for the organization. It is not enough for IT alone to consider itself successful at what it does. IT needs to provide real value to the organization that directly achieves business outcomes that the organization wants to achieve and should be able to deal with the ever changing needs and demands of the organizations and their customers. IT should also be capable of demonstrating how it provides business value to the organization to ensure that IT is positioned within the organization as a core strategic asset. How does IT achieve this? The simple answer is for IT to provide services that are required, can deliver value for money which is perceived by users and customers as providing value and by retiring services that do not, or no longer, provide value. IT needs to be able to show the organization the services that are provided in a format that is understood by the organization, as opposed to services described and presented in technical detail.

Imagine a restaurant with no menu. How is the customer to know what can be ordered? How does the chef know what to make with the raw ingredients that are available? How does one restaurant differentiate itself from another? How can the restaurant be profitable if customers do not know what is on offer and management cannot understand the cost of providing their services? Unlike the traditional restaurant menu, the service catalog offers much more to the organization than just a menu of available services. The service catalog provides IT with the capability to showcase to the organization the services that IT provides but also the business process and customer's services that are supported and provided by IT. The service catalog provides users and customers with the means of understanding what services they can actually use. Different views of the service catalog can provide service details and information in a format that is understood by the relevant audience.

How is ERZ broader than a catalog?

The service catalog is the only part of the overall service portfolio that can recover costs or earn profits. The relative cost of services can be identified easier if services can be broken down into reusable components. IT services that can be shared by multiple customers can be identified and economies of scale can lead to potential savings for the organization and lower costs to customers. Using the supplier catalog alone, consolidation of multiple suppliers providing the same services can be achieved, thus reducing the overall cost to the organization. The service catalog provides the platform for IT to charge the organization for their use of services provided in a fair and equitable manner.

The service catalog supports Business Impact Analysis (BIA). A major function of IT is to keep services operational and running during the times that services are required. Identifying potential impact to current live services is important to ensure that services are not affected when introducing changes to the live environment.

ITIL is now based around the service lifecycle. Central to this lifecycle are services. The service catalog plays a key role in the documenting and management of services within the organization and the actionable service catalogs provide the ability to reduce the cost of IT support and decrease manual intervention via automated workflows that support business processes. Customer actionable catalogs allow organizations to reach new markets at reduced costs.

1.3   Business benefits of the service catalog

The following is a list of benefits that can be attributable to the service catalog. All these benefits have a positive effect towards demonstrating return on investment back to the organization. The return provided can be from financial savings or can be provided indirectly via maximizing effectiveness and efficiencies within the organization. Any element of the service catalog that can reduce manual labor may provide a financial return on investment, though this has to be calculated. Having an IT service catalog can reduce lost time spent looking for information by IT support staff.

The service catalog:
* promotes IT into the role of a service provider that is service focused as opposed to technology centric
* facilitates IT to be run like a business and to allocate costs, or service charges, to specific departments within the organization
* reduces IT operational costs by not only providing services that are required but only to the agreed levels of capacity and availability
* reduces IT operational costs by identifying and eliminating IT service waste
* reduces IT service and process inefficiencies
* provides a platform to develop a clearer understanding of business requirements and challenges that must be faced
* provides a platform to improve the understanding of business requirements and issues that are experienced
* allows users and customers to choose the correct service for their needs
* provides the foundation for formal service level management and service catalog management
* improves the relationships and communications between IT and the business, within IT and between users and customers
* assists IT to market itself and build relationships throughout the business
* creates a platform to identify changes in demand. Requirements and demands are identified, understood and provisioned accordingly
* positively promotes a change in the way services are used (consumed)
* acts as a catalyst to drive improved internal and external communications
* increases customer satisfaction
* identifies critical business systems, thus allowing resources to be allocated when needed e.g. during high demand peaks or to prioritize incident resolution
* increases awareness and visibility for IT service provision

These are just some of the benefits that can be realized from the service catalog. Additional benefits are contained within the following chapters.

1.4   We need a service catalog. Make it happen!

Having looked at reasons why the service catalog is necessary, at some point in time the task of creating a service catalog will hopefully be identified. Inevitably, someone (hopefully senior management) within the organization at some point identifies the need to know and understand what exactly the IT department does, what it provides to the business and its customers, and how it supports users. They may also identify the need to actually charge for the services being provided in order to recover costs or to control the use patterns of services based on current demand and changing demand needs. If they have an understanding of ITIL, then the requirement may be identified as "needing a service catalog". So far things are straight forward. This requirement eventually lands on a manager's desk that has just been given responsibility for the simple task of putting together the service catalog. Seems straightforward, all that is needed is to draw up a list of what IT does and we are half way there. Not quite. In effect this approach is likely to lead to an inefficient and ineffective service catalog that offers neither value nor Return on Investment (ROI) and will most likely contribute to wasting a lot of people's time, resources, efforts and money.

There is certainly a need for guidance to ensure that an organization can:
- maximize the efforts of those involved
- get it right from the start
- design and implement a useable service catalog that is part of the service portfolio
- ensure the design and implementation will provide benefit to the business and customers
- ensure cost benefits and economies of scale are achieved

true – service catalog should be part of the service portfolio

In looking into how to go about this task there are a number of situations that can be faced:
- there is too much information about a subject and it is difficult to know what is what
- there is too little information about the subject
- wrong information is available about the subject

Suddenly the task seems not as straightforward as originally thought. Throughout this book guidance will be provided that will help the reader to understand what the service catalog is, how it fits within the service portfolio, what the different service catalog types are and most importantly of all how to achieve a quality and effective service catalog,

1.5 Qualifications and standards

This section explores existing qualifications and standards for service catalogs and initiatives to develop (open) standards.

1.5.1 ITIL Service Catalogue qualification

Service Catalogue is a complementary qualification to the ITIL V3 scheme, recommended by IQC, itSMFI's International Qualification and Certification Subcommittee. Service Catalogue is an APMG-International qualification. APMG-International is a global Examination Institute (EI) accredited by The APM Group which is OGC's official accreditation body. Service Catalogue is a "foundation plus" qualification based on Blooms Taxonomy levels 2-4. This means it has a higher difficulty level than a standard Foundation exam, but is not as challenging as an Intermediate-level exam. Obtaining the qualification will give candidates 1.5 credits towards the ITIL V3 Expert certification. The following information is taken from the APMG-UK website[1].

---

1   Service Catalog. *http://www.apmgroup.co.uk/ServiceCatalogue/ServiceCatalogue.asp.* APM Group 2009.

"Service Catalogue is a new qualification, complementary to the ITIL V3 suite. It looks at new ways to control demand, publish and track service pricing and cost, and automate service request management and fulfillment. The service catalogue provides a clear view of what services IT provides and how IT adds value for the money allocated. It provides a method to request or order the services that are published. The Service Catalogue enables good governance in that the key terms, conditions, and controls defined in the Service Catalogue are integrated into the service delivery processes of the organization. It enables an organization to better plan, deliver and support services while accurately costing and pricing services.

Studies show that implementing a role-driven, online, searchable catalogue with standardized services can convert costly requests for information, status, how-to and new service calls into zero-cost web-based user self-service. The Service Catalogue looks at common activities such as ordering of PC/desktop, telecommunication, collaboration, and support services, which can produce measurable results and assures consistent service pricing and quality.

Service Catalogue also looks at ways to help reduce cycle time; implementing workflow can reduce the time it takes to fulfill services, saving numerous hours per request. Organizations can thus reallocate precious staff time to more strategic initiatives.

The service catalogue certification is aimed at those with an ITIL Foundation certificate (or above) who have an interest in learning more about how a Service Catalogue could benefit their business."

To be eligible to take the Service Catalogue qualification, candidates should fulfill the following requirements:
- Have attained the ITIL Foundation Certificate, preferably the current version.
- Have attended at least 18 hours of instruction (exclusive of breaks, lunches and the exam) with an accredited training organization or e-learning based on this syllabus, as part of a formal, approved training course.
- It is strongly recommended that candidates have exposure to basic Service Catalogue concepts and related work experience of around two years.

It is also recommended that students complete at least 12 hours of personal study in preparation for the examination. Upon achievement of the qualification, candidates will be able to:
- analyze and adopt new ways to control demand
- publish and track service pricing and cost
- automate service request management and fulfillment

Training courses in Service Catalogue, including the exam, will be available through Accredited Training Organizations (ATOs). Candidates will need to contact the individual training organizations for details of locations, fees and formats for training courses. APMG does not hold information on the ATOs' individual courses but they ensure the training provided by ATOs meets APMG's required standards, in accordance with the quality standard EN45011. Any training company wishing to offer the Service Catalogue qualification must be accredited by APMG-International.

The ITIL V3 Qualification Scheme introduces a modular credit system for each of the V3 certifications. All modules are given a credit value, and candidates meeting the requisite entry criteria and accumulating the required number of credits (22) can apply for ITIL Expert level certification. Certifications from earlier ITIL versions (V1 and V2) are also recognized within the system, together with qualifications endorsed as complementary to the V3 qualification portfolio. The purpose of the ITIL Credit Profiler is to advise ITIL candidates of the total credit value they have attained within the scheme and to provide general guidance on potential routes for further study based on candidate educational or certification objectives.

The ITIL Credit Profiler System is shown in figure 1.1. Over time it is expected that additional complementary certifications will be added.

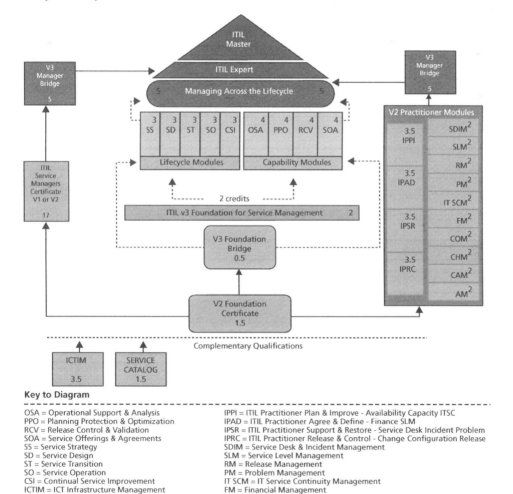

Key to Diagram

OSA = Operational Support & Analysis
PPO = Planning Protection & Optimization
RCV = Release Control & Validation
SOA = Service Offerings & Agreements
SS = Service Strategy
SD = Service Design
ST = Service Transition
SO = Service Operation
CSI = Continual Service Improvement
ICTIM = ICT Infrastructure Management

IPPI = ITIL Practitioner Plan & Improve - Availability Capacity ITSC
IPAD = ITIL Practitioner Agree & Define - Finance SLM
IPSR = ITIL Practitioner Support & Restore - Service Desk Incident Problem
IPRC = ITIL Practitioner Release & Control - Change Configuration Release
SDIM = Service Desk & Incident Management
SLM = Service Level Management
RM = Release Management
PM = Problem Management
IT SCM = IT Service Continuity Management
FM = Financial Management
COM = Configuration Management
CHM = Change Management
CAM = Capacity Management
AM = Availability Management

Figure 1.1 ITIL Credit Profiler System (Source: APMG[2])

While the service catalog complementary certification is a welcome addition, there is no defined standard (as of yet) for service catalogs although it should be noted that an organization does not need to comply with a standard in order to have a quality service catalog in place. What fits one organization by way of definition, design, implementation and management may not suit another organization. Also what is defined in one organization may not easily be applicable to another. Books, like this one, aim to help organizations understand basic principles and provide information that will help the organization achieve a favorable outcome.

1.5.2 Service Portfolio and Catalog Language (SPACL)

A consortium has been formed in order to collaborate on the development of a vendor neutral open standard definition for service catalog offerings, and for exchanging service requests between Service Catalog systems. This consortium is called the Service Portfolio and Catalog Language (SPACL) and they have a SPACL Public Review Forum available online[3]. They are also responsible for the formation of an industry standards group to define standards for the exchange of service portfolio and service catalog information between different systems and vendors. This standard will be known as the Service Portfolio and Catalog Language (SPACL). It is the intention of the SPACL consortium to submit the specification to an industry standard group once it is matured. It remains to be seen how vendor neutral the initiative is but that is something beyond the scope of this book and something that you, the reader, can ascertain for yourself if it is something of concern. There should be enough information available on their website or from the group to allow the reader to make an informed decision on the matter.

The following is an extract from their website site[4]:

> The SPACL consortium is a collaboration of companies that have joined to develop a vendor-neutral open standard definition for Service Catalog offerings, and for exchanging service requests between Service Catalog systems. These definitions are key to enable service request operations between IT consumers, internal IT organizations, and external service providers – including cloud computing providers. It is the intention of the SPACL consortium to submit the specification to an industry standard group once it is matured.
>
> **SPACL Goals**
> ITIL V3 makes the service catalog central to IT service management implementations. In fact, 22 ITIL processes depend on the service catalog. IT organizations have very high expectations for their service catalog. Unfortunately, many struggle when they go to build their service catalog. There are multiple reasons for this, among them is the lack of standards for defining content, lack of implementation guidance, and difficulty in managing business objectives around catalog implementations.

---

3   Service Portfolio and Catalog Language - Public review site for SPACL documents, *http://www.spacl.info/*, SPACL 2009.
4   Service Portfolio and Catalog Language - Public review site for SPACL documents *http://www.spacl.info/forum/topics/spacl-announcement*, SPACL 2009.
     Service Portfolio and Catalog Language - Public review site for SPACL documents *http://www.spacl.info/notes/SPACL_Goals/*, SPACL 2009.

The SPACL Consortium is actively working to build:
- *an open-standard definition of Service Offerings and Service Requests that is vendor and tool agnostic*
- *provide sufficient rigor to guide customers content generation*
- *clear set of content and data structures so customers can succeed*
- *a definitional model so catalog development is decoupled from operations*
- *content can be defined independently of how it will be use operationally*
- *this simplifies projects, enriches the usability of the catalog*
- *rigorous, normative schema that enables automated exchange of definitions*
- *portfolio can send service definitions to CMDB, Provisioning, Finance, HR, Billing, PPM, etc*

The SPACL specification
The SPACL specification provides a clear set of XML-based schema definitions, content and data structures so that IT organizations and service providers can succeed at implementing and exchanging Service Catalog and Service Portfolio definitions. SPACL is designed to be extensible so customers and vendors can add new elements and attributes while maintaining interoperability.

1.5.3 United Nations Standard Products and Services Code (UNSPSC)

The United Nations have developed a standard (of sorts) in relation to the classification of products and services. While this does not map directly to IT, it may be of interest from a taxonomy point of view and can be found at the following location: http://www.unspsc.org/

The United Nations Standard Products and Services Code (UNSPSC®) provides an open, global multi-sector standard for efficient, accurate classification of products and services. Search the code on this website to locate commodity codes that can be used by your company.

The UNSPSC offers a single global classification system that can be used for:
- *company-wide visibility of spend analysis*
- *cost-effective procurement optimization*
- *full exploitation of electronic commerce capabilities*
- *you may browse and download the current version of the code at no cost*

Why should businesses classify products & services?[5]

Classifying products and services with a common coding scheme facilitates commerce between buyers and sellers and is becoming mandatory in the new era of electronic commerce. Large companies are beginning to code purchases in order to analyze their spending.

---

5   Frequently Asked Questions, *http://www.unspsc.org/FAQs.asp#whyclassify*, UNSPC 2009.

of info may be
of interest to
Lora ✱
/

By classifying their products & services, businesses can assist their customers with:

- *Finding and purchasing - a product and service coding convention brings many benefits to the purchasing function of a company.*
- *Product discovery - a common naming convention allows computer systems to automatically list similar products under a single category. When a person is searching for the category, he or she finds precisely the things being discovered and nothing else.*
- *Facilitates expenditure analysis - when every purchase transaction of an enterprise is tagged with a common set of product identifiers, purchasing managers are able to analyze enterprise expenditures.*
- *Control and uniformity across the company - codes bring a single, uniform view of all expenditures in a company. It ties together all departments and divisions, including business functions such as purchasing and settlement.*

The United Nations Standard Products and Services Code® (UNSPSC®) provides an open, global multi-sector standard for efficient, accurate classification of products and services. Search the code on this website to locate commodity codes that can be used by your company.

2 Definition and basic concepts

In order to begin our journey into the world of the service catalog, it is important to have a full understanding of a number of key concepts and definitions from the start. The goal of this chapter is to explain terminology and concepts that are used throughout this book and will cover the general terms, definitions and concepts that are to be found in the context of service catalogs. A number of these terms and concepts are described in detail within this chapter while others are described elsewhere throughout this book.

While the focus of this book is the service catalog the service catalog's position within the service portfolio will be discussed. As the service catalog is a major component of the service portfolio, the information provided will enhance understanding. Also, anyone wishing to create a service portfolio will benefit from this information.

2.1 Users and customers

For the purpose of this book, the author will refer to the organizations employees as *users*. Those external to the organization, who are willing to purchase products and services from the organization, will be referred to as *customers*. However some organizations operate a cross-charge policy and in effect, the users become internal customers, who, in the context of this book will be referred to as users.

2.2 Utility and warranty

Throughout the book there will be repeating references made in regard to services delivering value to customers and in supporting outcomes that the organization want to achieve. ITIL uses figure 2.1 to demonstrate the logic of value creation through services. The ITIL Service Strategy book introduces the concepts of *utility* and *warranty* that are referenced throughout the five core ITIL books.

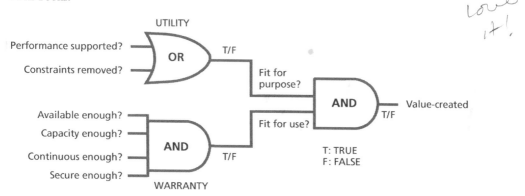

Figure 2.1 Value creation through services (Source: OGC)

The ITIL glossary quite simply states the following:

> *(ITIL Glossary) "The business value of an IT service is created by the combination of service utility (what the service does) and service warranty (how well it does it).*

Utility[6] is perceived by the customer from the attributes of the service that have a positive effect on the performance of tasks associated with desired outcomes. Removal or relaxation of constraints on performance is also perceived as a positive effect. Warranty is derived from the positive effect being available when needed, in sufficient capacity or magnitude, and dependability in terms of continuity and security. Put another way *utility* is what the customers gets (fit for purpose) and *warranty* is how it is delivered (fit for use). ITIL states that the value perceived by the customer is dependent on supporting the performance of the service or removing constraints that can affect service performance AND by ensuring that the service is available as expected, can handle changing demand requirements, and has adequate security provisions. Value is not perceived if the service can provide appropriate levels of utility but not appropriate levels of warranty and vice versa.

In the context of this book what the ITIL glossary refers to as an "IT service" can actually relate to any of the service types that will be discussed throughout this book. This is because the value of the service that is created is seen through the eyes of the user/customer perspective. As users within the organization will use business services and customers will use customer services, referencing just IT services is far too narrow a context from which to work from.

2.3   What is a service?

There is a lot of misunderstanding as to what exactly a service is, and what components make up a service. This confusion is not confined to organizations. Practitioners, consultants and vendors have struggled with defining services, not in definition, but in the context of what is perceived as a service in an organization and how best to represent these services.

An area where many people find themselves in disagreement is with regards to the definitions of what constitutes a service, never mind what an (IT) system or an (IT) service might actually be. In one sense it may not matter if we disagree. One may argue that whether we call it an (IT) system or an (IT) service is not as important as actually mapping the service accurately and that this is just an exercise in taxonomy. It is necessary to define and understand services but also it is necessary to decompose services into their various components in order to better understand the service end-to-end and to:
- build accurate service maps piece by piece
- price and cost services more accurately
- report on services at different levels

---

6   The definition of utility and warranty is taken from the ITIL Service Strategy book (OGC)

- utilize the different parts of the service catalog effectively
- develop a clearer picture of what it is that IT does in support of the business (from the most obvious to the most obscure)
- understand how the organization actually relies on IT to do business

In the publication "IT Service Management Global Best Practices, Volume 1"[7], Karen Ferris has the following to say about the subject in her best practice guidance entitled "Out of one silo and into another":

> *"There are so many organizations still trying to determine what they mean by a 'service' that is holding them back from determining service ownership and associated roles and responsibilities. Until one can define what is meant by a 'service', end-to-end service ownership cannot be established. Once this has been done, service owners can be put in place to own the end-to-end services and ensure that they meet the needs of the business by delivering business value and outcomes that the customer wants."*

Over the years a number of best, and good, practice frameworks, standards, Bodies of Knowledge (BOKs) and toolkits have been developed or published and are widely available. Some are proprietary and vendor specific and others are vendor neutral instead offering general guidance and best practice that can be applied irrespective of the technology used and the structure of the organization. Most come at a cost while a few are freely available or at least supplemental reference material is provided freely. Standards have also been developed for organizations to use. The following are a number of frameworks and standards in general use, but there are many more available. Additional information on these can be found in Appendix D:

- ITIL®
- CobiT®
- MOF
- ISO/IEC 20000:2005
- USMBOK™ *okay, and I got this recently*
- ISM™

Throughout this book, references will be made to these frameworks and the definitions that they provide for a number of key areas. This is to provide the reader with a broad overview of key concepts in regards to how they are defined in the different knowledge domains. Currently, there is no defined standard for service catalogs and therefore different knowledge domains can and will use different definitions. *is this still true? would Mary know?*

---

7   Ferris, Karen (2008). "Out of one silo and into another", *IT Service Management Global Best Practices, Volume 1.* Van Haren Publishing 2008. ISBN-9087531001.

Framework definitions of a service

Framework	Definitions of service
Service Delivery (previous ITIL version)	One or more IT systems which enable a business process.
(Service Design)	A means of delivering value to customers by facilitating outcomes customers want to achieve without the ownership of specific costs and risks. In taking this further the ITIL Service Design book (page 62) states the following: (Service Design) "So what is a service? The question is not as easy to answer as it may first appear, and many organizations have failed to come up with a clear definition in an IT context. IT staff often confuse a "service" as perceived by the customer with an IT system. In many cases one "service" can be made up of other "services" (and so on), which are themselves made up of one or more IT systems within an overall infrastructure including hardware, software, networks, together with environments, data and applications. A good starting point is often to ask customers which IT services they use and how those services map onto and support their business processes. Customers often have a greater clarity of what they believe a service to be. Each organization needs to develop a policy of what is a service and how it is defined and agreed within their own organization."
MOF	Customer Service SMF A collection of features and functions that enable a business process.
ISO/IEC 20000-1:2005	Although IT uses products in the delivery of IT services, it is now considered to be a typical services domain. So what is the difference between a product and a service? This can be expressed in terms of the following characteristics: – services are intangible – services are produced and consumed at the same time – services are very variable – the user takes part in the production of the service – satisfaction is subjective
USMBOK	(Introduction to Service) As the legal definition states, a service is generally described as work performed by one group that benefits another. The following simplistic definition taken from an established reference (1) will form the basis for the definition of a service in this document: A service is any act or performance that one person can offer to another that is essentially intangible and does not result in any transfer of ownership. The value of the service to the customer is through the results achieved through its use - the outcome. The importance of the service to the provider is through the satisfaction and value it provides the customer, the revenue it generates for the provider, versus the cost of production. Its distribution and use may be tied to a physical product. (1) Marketing Management 7th Edition, Philip Kotler, 1991
ISM	A service is functioning functionality. The ISM definition is based on the ISM Infrastructure Paradigm, showing the decomposition of a service into a variety of infrastructure elements (the "functionality"), where various quality terms (the "functioning") apply.

Table 2.1 Framework definitions of service

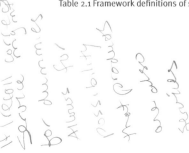

The author would like to provide the following definition of what is a **service**:

> *A **service** is any act or performance that one person can offer to another, that is intangible, produced at the moment of delivery and does not result in transfer of ownership. Service value and quality is based on customer perception, where satisfaction is based on outcomes and is subjective. Three main services are:*
> *Customer service: services provided to the organizations customers*
> *Business service: support business processes that enable the organization to achieve its desired outcomes*
> *IT service: provides IT capabilities that support and deliver business and customer services*

So, if the context of a service is not new, and if the available frameworks define what they see a service as, then why is it so difficult for organizations:
- to understand what a service is in the IT and business arenas
- to define what services exist in the context of an organization
- to build a service catalog that is fit for purpose and fit for use

Is it to do with the fact that:
- service definition has been defined in too broad a context
- standards, frameworks and best practices have not provided guidance on the *how* element in designing and building service models or service catalogs
- services can, and will be, perceived differently from one person to another
- little focus has been placed on how the organization is to:
  - *develop* their understanding of their organizations services
  - *design* a service mapping relevant to the organization's offerings
  - *deliver* a service catalog that is relevant and fit for purpose

An important point to note is that it is essential for organizations to state clearly how they define services within the context of their organization. This includes the definition of the service and the service model i.e. how the different services map together. The previous definitions should help with understanding what a service is. Failing to correctly define services can lead to a service catalog that is ineffective and provides no real value to any part of the organization. If services are not defined with the relevant audience in mind, they will not be understood so how could they be viewed as being strategically important to the organization? The following sections will help with understanding what the main service types are which should help clarify things further. If the question still remains "what is a service", an examination of the service catalog should help reveal some more important aspects to this question in regards to finding the answer.

2.4   The service catalog

This section explores existing definitions of the service catalog and integrates the several elements of the service catalog in a final basic definition.

While the mainstream Bodies of Knowledge (BOKs) that exist in the public domain define the service catalog they do not provide enough practical information and guidance that shed light on how to achieve the following:

- understand the service catalog
- plan the service catalog
- design the service catalog
- develop the service catalog
- manage the service catalog
- maintain the service catalog

The core ITIL books, in particular Service Strategy and Service Design, provide details about the service catalog. They provide details about what the service catalog is while allowing for complementary books, such as this one, to delve into more detail and provide specific information on the subject. So, if this book is about understanding service catalogs in more detail and how they can be developed for an organization, what exactly is a service catalog?

To shed some light, the ITIL glossary has the following information:

(Service Design) Service Catalog: "A database or structured Document with information about all Live IT Services, including those available for Deployment. The Service Catalogue is the only part of the Service Portfolio published to Customers, and is used to support the sale and delivery of IT Services. The Service Catalogue includes information about deliverables, prices, contact points, ordering and request Processes. See Contract Portfolio."

The ITIL Service Strategy book offers more insight into the subject of the service catalog. Have a look at chapters three and four for some specific information. The following are some relevant extracts from this section in the book which will be expanded on in detail throughout this book. This is an example of the information that ITIL and other frameworks offer.

Framework	Definitions
Service Strategy	The service catalog is the subset of the service portfolio visible to customers. It consists of services presently active in the service operation phase and those approved to be readily offered to current and prospective customers. It serves as a service order and demand channeling mechanism. It acts as the acquisition portal for customers, including pricing and service-level commitments, and terms and conditions for service provisioning. It is in the service catalog that services are decomposed into components; it is where assets, process and systems are introduced with entry points and terms for their use and provisioning.
MOF	Business-IT Alignment SMF A comprehensive list of services, including priorities of the business and corresponding SLAs.

[handwritten margin note: Bill's briefly allowed for a service catalog (view) for developers]

Framework	Definitions
ISO/IEC 20000-1:2005	(The code of practice): Service catalog A service catalog should define all services. It can be referenced from the SLA and should be used to hold material considered volatile for the SLA itself. *[handwritten: ?, what does this mean?]* The service catalog should be maintained and kept up to date. Note: The service catalog can include generic information such as: a) the name of the service b) targets, for example, time to respond or install a printer, time to re-instate a service after a major failure c) contact points d) service hours and exceptions e) security arrangements The service catalogue is a key document for setting customer expectation and should be easily accessible, and widely available to both customers and support staff.
USMBOK	The service catalog *[handwritten: so here the service catalog may equate to the portfolio — that is not consistent w/ some other usage]* A service catalog markets an authorized service portfolio, or subset. A service catalog consists of one or more descriptions of current service offerings and optionally, future service capabilities. A service catalog is defined in terms understood by its intended customer audience and is the basis for requesting and negotiating service, and desired levels of service. A service catalog entry is the first stage of influencing and setting service level expectations.
ISM	A service catalog provides a description of (partial) services that can be provided by the service provider, in part or in combination. A specific choice of these services can be agreed in an SLA.

Table 2.2 Service catalog definitions

So there we have it: *[handwritten: ERZ?, does ERZ have suitable structure/ governance (e.g., service naming conventions, etc.)]*

*The **service catalog** is a repository that contains information about services or it is a comprehensive list of services. It defines all services. It is an ordering mechanism with pricing. It is where services are decomposed into components. It sets customer expectations. It is the entry point of influencing and settling service levels.*

Is that all we need to know? Could it be that simple?

A list of services on its own does not provide any real benefit to the business. On its own a list of IT services does not allow:

- end-users and customers to interact and order services
- the business to understand how IT enables their operations
- chargeback for services consumed
- the ability for IT to know what it delivers in support of the business
- the business to understand its reliance on IT in order to be able to carry out key, critical and core business functions and objectives
- service impact assessments

Definitions serve a purpose but only go so far. Bodies of Knowledge have a vast spectrum to cover and may not provide such level of detail. In recent years vendors have closed the gap in providing information on the subject. It should be observed that some may also have clouded the issue, as tools and practices adopted by some vendors may provide neither a consistent definition of services, nor the service catalog.

Service catalog repository considerations

The information that the service catalogs hold and the relationships between the different service catalog types is key to the service catalog structure. There are a number of realistic options available, some of which can include:

- spreadsheets
- documents
- Configuration Management Database (CMDB)/Configuration Management System (CMS)[8]
- service management systems
- service catalog/specialist software applications

These options are discussed in more detail in chapter 7.

ITIL is heavily focused on services, on the service lifecycle and on the value that services are delivering to the organization and their customers. Paramount to this is the service catalog. The service catalog is generally referred to in the singular. Therefore, it is quite common for people to develop a single service catalog or to believe that they must develop a single catalog. However, the service catalog is not just one entity. There are a number of service catalog types that can exist within an organization.

The following section provides details on not just the two catalogs described in ITIL but details eight distinct, but complementary, service catalog types represented within the Service Portfolio Pyramid - explained later in this chapter - and will deal with the commonly asked question: "How do we represent these service catalog types?"

2.4.1 Service types and catalog types

There are many different types of services that can exist in an organization. Each organization is different and each organization will use and offer different services to fulfill the needs of their users and customers. Equally, there are a number of basic service types that exist through many organizations. These, if used constructively, will form the basis of a service catalog that can apply to, and have relevance within, many different organizations. At a minimum the service catalog should define services for the following service types:

- IT systems
- IT services
- business services
- customer services

Actionable service catalogs include:

- business actionable services
- customer actionable services

Optional catalogs that provide value will include:

- product catalog
- supplier catalog
- professional services catalog

---

8   The CMS which was introduced in ITIL V3 extends/integrates the concept of the CMDB.

Figure 2.2 shows how all these service catalog types are logically linked together. Using this taxonomy allows for the different service types to be recorded and presented to and understood by the relevant audience. In theory the service catalog could be a single repository. However, the reality is that the service catalog may actually span multiple repositories. These service catalog types will be discussed in more detail in chapter three and a service catalog design schematic is provided in chapter 5.

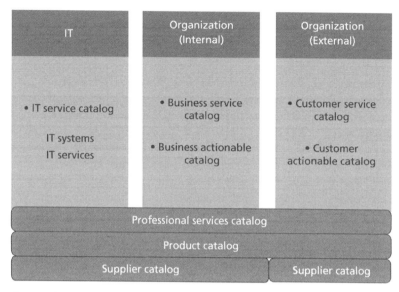

Figure 2.2 The different service catalog types and their target audience

2.5   Service records

The term *service record* is used within this chapter and throughout this book. Therefore it is important at this juncture to explain the concept of service records.

A service record is a form that contains specific details about each service and its associated attributes. This is in much the same way that a CI record contains information about a CI and the attributes of the CI. The service record can be created within a spreadsheet, a document, a service management application, a specific service catalog application or even a bespoke purpose built system. Obviously there are drawbacks to creating service records in documents, the main one being that the information exists in isolation from other service records with no direct links. Reporting on services is also manual and time consuming. Spreadsheets offer a little more functionality but have limitations and may not support anything more than basic service mappings.

A service record:
- holds information about the service
- is related to other service records which forms the basis for service mapping

- links to related documentation, for example SLAs, Operational Level Agreements (OLAs), work instructions
- identifies the status of the service which denotes its place in the service lifecycle

It should be possible to create the IT catalog within the CMDB/CMS by using CI records or forms and classifying them as IT service records. This is a way to benefit from using an existing CMDB/CMS within the organization and to leverage economies of scale by not having to invest in a specific or standalone service catalog application. It would be necessary for the CMDB/CMS to be capable of making relationships between the records in order to map out the services. IT system records are related to IT service records in order to create a mapping for the IT services. IT service records are related to business service records in order to create a mapping of business services and their supporting IT services.

In the author's experience, a lot of CMDB applications are well capable of creating CI relationships and support the use of service records to map services to each other, while some CMDB applications are not. If the CMDB is to be considered an appropriate repository for creating service records then be sure to check the CMDB capabilities to ensure that good relationships can not only be made but also displayed in an appropriate format as some CMDB products are good at relationships but poor on how they represent these relationships back to the user.

Table 2.3 shows some of the more basic information that should be stored within the different service catalog records. The listing provides some idea of the basic information that should be recorded for the different types of service catalogs. Recording too much information will give information overload and require a great deal of administration to keep relevant and up to date. Recording too little will be of minimal or even no use. Not only does the organization need to know what services exist, they also need to know enough about those services in order to understand, provide, support and maintain each service. Therefore there is the need to record such information about each service.

IT service catalog	Business service catalog	Customer service catalog	Business & customer actionable service catalogs[9]	Information access
These help define and filter the service				This information may be presented to the users of the service
Service name	Service name	Service name	Service name	
Description	Description	Description	Description	
Status	Status	Status	Status	
Service type	Service type	Service type	Service type	
Classification	Classification	Classification	Classification	
Service objective	Service objective	Service objective	Service objective	

IT service catalog	Business service catalog	Customer service catalog	Business & customer actionable service catalogs[9]	Information access
These help understand how and where the service is supported & who has access				This information should be available to support personnel and management
Service owner	Service owner	Service owner	Service owner	
Link to OLA	Link to SLA	Link to contracts	Link to SLA	
Level 1 support	Level 1 support	Initial point of contact	Initial point of contact	
Level 2 support	Level 2 support	Support hours	Support hours	
Level 3 support	Level 3 support	Entitlement	Entitlement	
Level 1 support hours	Level 1 support hours			
Level 2 support hours	Level 2 support hours			
Level 3 support hours	Level 3 support hours			
Link to policies & procedures	Link to policies & procedures	Link to policies & procedures	Link to policies & procedures	
Supplier	Supplier	Supplier	Supplier	
Service configuration details				Service record is generally linked to this information
CI relationships (from the CMDB/CMS)	Service relationships	Service relationships	Service relationships	
Link to technical & project documentation (from the CMDB/CMS)	Link to business specifications	Link to customer specifications	Link to business & customer specifications	
			Workflows & design documents	
A few extra fields - this is where it gets organizational specific				This information should be available to support personnel and management
Agreed availability hours	Agreed availability hours	Agreed availability hours	Agreed availability hours	
Critical availability periods	Critical availability periods	Critical availability periods	Critical availability periods	
Service maintenance windows	Service maintenance windows	Service maintenance windows	Service maintenance windows	
Backup and recovery procedures	Backup and recovery procedures	Backup and recovery procedures	Backup and recovery procedures	
Charging arrangements	Charging arrangements	Charging arrangements	Charging arrangements	

Table 2.3 Basic information to be recorded in the different service catalog types

There is no limit to the information that can be stored in a service record but bear in mind that too much information can be as useless as too little. If starting out with service records remember that less is more. It is easier to grow service records and add more information in over time than it is to reduce the data that is being recorded. The same applies to the CMDB. Reengineering and reducing the information stored within either the service catalog or the CMDB is a challenging task. It is not impossible, but there are a lot of considerations, vested interests and hurdles that need to be dealt with before the tasks and activities can be completed. Regardless of where the service records are stored, they must be placed under change control. This is to ensure that the information that they contain is updated as services change or are modified and also to ensure that the data contained within the service records remain accurate and valid.

An example of a basic service record for an IT service is provided in figure 2.3. It has many attributes and fields that are similar to what should be recorded against a business service, a customer service or an IT service. The *service type* is what distinguishes the service records from one another, and based on the classification, the relevant fields and attributes can be made available to the person completing the service catalog record. Recording service catalog records within a specific application will make it more likely to for information to be added in a controlled way, by using predefined drop down lists, requesting specific information and setting text only or numeric fields. It also facilitates reporting on the service records. How many services are in use? How many services are provided by IT? Is service charging taking place, and if so how does the organization know what to charge for? What IT services make up a business service and vice versa? The information provided in this example shows some of the basic yet important information from the previous table that should be recorded. In reality the service record form may have additional sections, presented over different tabs, provided by a different looking interface.

There are a number of sections within this example which are described below.

General information
Provides general details about the service.
- *Status* denotes where the service is within its lifecycle. In this case the service is operational and is in use – Live.
- *Service type* denotes that this service record contains the details and information for an IT service.
- *Classification* is used to group and filter the service records and to report on them.

Support information
Provides support information about the service. Links to documents are included.

Service levels
Service levels provide details about the agreed levels of service as per the service requirements and any agreed service level targets. If an SLA exists for the service then details can be included here or the SLA document link can be included. In this example the agreed availability hours may seem high but the reality is that an organization is likely to want to have their communications services operations and available all the time. Service level agreements are discussed further in chapter 6 and Appendix E contains an example of a service level agreement template.

General information		Support information		Service levels	
Service name	Instant messaging	*Service owner*	Mark O'Loughlin	*Agreed availability hours*	24*7 365
Status	Live	*Link to OLA*	http://docserv1/OLA-IM.doc	*Critical availability periods*	Financial year end
Service type	IT service	*Level 1 support*	Service desk	*Service maintenance windows*	1st Sunday of every month between 03.00 - 05:00 hrs GMT
Classification	Communciation services	*Level 1 support hours for service*	24*7 365	*Backup and recover procedures*	http://docserv1/IMBP.doc
Description / Service objective	Allows all users within the organisation to communicate with each other using a desktop client.	*Level 2 support*	Technical group	*Charging arrangements*	Bundled with and charged as part of the 'Communication services'
		Level 2 support hours for service	07:00hrs-19:00hrs GMT otherwise on call	*Service last reviewed*	20-Oct-09
		Level 3 support	None		
		Level 3 support hours for service	Not applicable		

Service map				Process relationships	
Up level services		*Down level services*		Modules	ID Number
Customer service	Business service	IT system name	Related CIs		10301 Request client install
	Communication services	MS Exchange	Exchange server-1	Service requests	27036 Request for new user
			Exchange server-2		282318 Request for new user
			Messaging server-1	Incidents	10356 Client not logging in
		Active directory	Directory server-1		10391 Error
			Storage server-1	Problems	3287 Error code 121
			Messaging server-1		8390 Roll out new client
			LAN switch-1	Change requests	9210 Make new features available
			Router-1		10175 Change in support hours

Figure 2.3 Example of a service catalog record for an IT service

The last two sections are the additional elements of the service catalog record that should be included within the service catalog record. These sections provide a critical link in mapping the service records together and relating the service to the ITIL processes used to support the services. This may not be feasible if the service records are recorded within word documents, spreadsheets or very simple application and service management tools.

Service map
This is the section that links together all the different service records that make up the service. In this example the CIs are shown with the IT systems that they are related to in order for those IT systems to function. The IT systems that are needed to provide this IT service are related to this service record. The business service that requires this IT service is also related. The relationships shown here are shown in a basic hierarchal manner. Some service catalogs provide an interface that shows these relationships in an actual map while others do not. The benefit of this is that it is easier to visualize how the service is constructed. Chapter 4 provides additional details about mapping services and chapter 5 includes a service catalog schematic that helps to visualize how services interconnect and join up.

Process relationships   – evolving over time
Another powerful element of a service catalog record is the ability to relate service requests, incidents, problems and change requests to each service record. Over time this allows for business

intelligence style reporting which can report on the issues that affect each service, which will have associated costs to support and fix the requests that are logged for each service, showing demand patterns increasing or decreasing over time and change activity taking place to the service or a related service type, helping to identify potential impact and single points of failure. This is very powerful information to have and is only possible if the service records can be related to these processes. Some service management systems will have this capability and some won't. Again, recording services within word documents or spreadsheets will not allow for this type of reporting to be possible.

2.6   The service portfolio

The previous sections have briefly looked at services and have identified the service types that will constitute the service catalog. However, the journey does not end there. The service catalog is actually a subset of the service portfolio. Therefore the service portfolio and the service catalog must interface with each other. Understanding these interfaces will help organizations get the most from their investment in both the service catalog and service the portfolio and to get one step closer to establishing the ITIL service lifecycle. Although this book is primarily focused on exploring the service catalog, this section contains information about the service portfolio and where the service catalog is positioned within the service portfolio. This leads us to the next question "So what exactly is the service portfolio?".

At a basic level the service portfolio:
* is an executive-level view that allows an organization to map their services to the business requirements
* is used to analyze where investment is needed or is being allocated
* can also assist with the allocation of resources, risk management and financial modeling
* can help prioritize investment decisions
* represents the ability of the organization to provide services to customer and market places
* represents commitments and investment made by the organization
* represents all services within the service lifecycle
* helps to identify and understand the true costs involved in service provision while the service catalog is concerned with the pricing of the service to users and customers

The service portfolio is defined as:

Framework	Service portfolio definitions
Service Strategy	The complete set of services that are managed by a service provider. The service portfolio is used to manage the entire lifecycle of all services, and includes three categories: service pipeline (proposed or in development); service catalog (live or available for deployment); and retired services. The service portfolio represents the commitments and investments made by a service provider across all customers and market spaces. It represents present contractual commitments, new service development, and ongoing service improvement plans initiated by continual service improvement. The portfolio also includes third-party services, which are an integral part of service offerings to customers. Some third-party services are visible to customers while others are not. ITIL provides figure 2.4 in the Service Strategy book to further expand on this concept.

Framework	Service portfolio definitions
MOF	Business-IT Alignment SMF An internal repository that defines IT services and categorizes them as currently in service, in queue to be developed, or in queue to be decommissioned. All services support a specific business process or function.
USMBOK	A service portfolio is a collection of services managed as an investment by the service provider organization to maximize the total beneficial value derived from its use of resources. USMBOK provides the following comparison between the service catalog and the service portfolio: A service catalog is NOT a service portfolio. A service portfolio is an approach to manage information system services as investments with profit and loss based perspective. A service catalog is a marketing tool for service portfolios. They coexist and a service catalog enables and supports a service portfolio.

Table 2.4 Framework definitions of service portfolio

good distinction

and presumably a service catalog(s) may be an item(s) w/in the service portfolio?

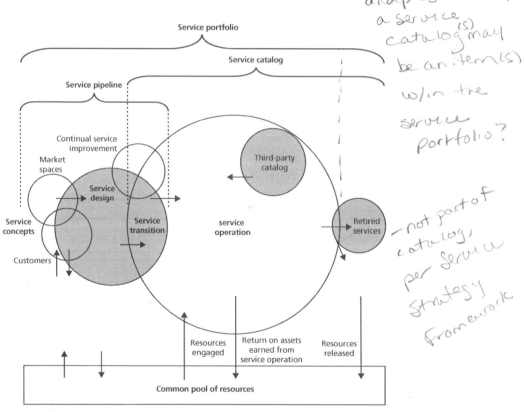

– not part of catalog, per Service Strategy Framework

Area of circle is proportional to resources currently engaged in the lifecycle phase (Service portfolio and financial management)

Figure 2.4 Service portfolio (Source: OGC)

The three elements of the ITIL service portfolio are briefly described as follows:

Element	Description
Service pipeline	Services proposed or in development
Service catalog	Services live or available for deployment
Retired services	Services no longer in use

Table 2.5 Three elements of the service portfolio (ITIL)

A simplified version of the service portfolio is represented in figure 2.5 (service lifecycle). These elements make up what is in effect the lifecycle of a service from cradle to grave, i.e. conception to retirement.

Figure 2.5 Simplified view of the service portfolio

So what does the service portfolio offer the organization above and beyond being a list of services that are being developed, live or retired? Why would an organization want to have a service portfolio? The service portfolio represents the commitments and investments made by a service provider / or the organization. It is the source of information regarding contractual commitments, new services that are under development and ongoing service improvements and describes services in terms of their business value. It is the main source of information regarding the requirements of new services which need to be designed carefully to ensure that they meet the needs of the uses and customers. The service portfolio helps the organization's management to prioritize investments and investment decisions in regards to what services should and should not be provisioned and to improve the allocation of resources in the design, build and operate stages of each service. The service portfolio acts as a platform to promote appropriate financial disciplines necessary to avoid investments that will not yield value. The following table provides details of basic activities of each service portfolio element and also includes suggested status codes that can be used to define where services are within the service lifecycle stage.

Element	Activities	Service status code
Service pipeline	• budgeting decisions • identify economies of scale from existing services • identification of Service Level Requirements (SLRs) (service design stage) • investment prioritization • understanding of costs involved in creating the service • business cases • risk analysis	• definition • analysis • approved • charter • design • in development • built • under testing • user acceptance t(UAT) • pre production

[handwritten margin note: I assume there may be other activities here]

Service catalog	• service charging • service maps • impact assessment • identify single point of failure • service offerings (actionable service catalog)	• in production *[handwritten: live]* • not in service
Retired services	• record of services no longer in use • shows past investments • can aid decisions on new service investments by understanding previous issues	• retired

Table 2.6 What does the service portfolio offer the organization?

As stated in the previous section the service status code can be used to denote which part of the service portfolio the service is residing in at that point in time. A number of unique service status codes can apply across the whole of the service portfolio. Some very basic service status codes are provided in table 2.6. Each status should be unique and should apply to only one of the three service catalog *[handwritten: portfolio]* elements. It is an exercise in itself to come up with service status codes that are unique and relevant for each of the three service portfolio elements but it is an exercise worth undertaking and doing correctly. Creating too many status codes may prove difficult to maintain and to keep up to date. Having too few codes may not provide a clear depiction of the services and where they are within the service portfolio.

ITIL's representation of the elements of a service portfolio and service catalog is shown in figure 2.6.

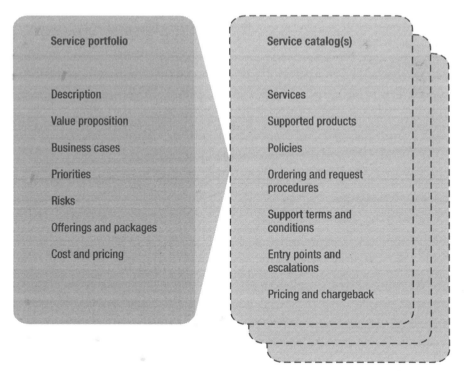

Figure 2.6 ITIL's representation of the elements of a service portfolio and service catalog (Source: OGC)

[handwritten: interesting]

ITIL focuses on the service lifecycle covering services from *cradle to grave* and recommends that the place to start from is to define the service portfolio. However, in reality, how many organizations start by defining a service portfolio? How many organizations are playing catch-up? How many organizations *don't get it* or worse still *don't care to get it?* Some general reasons organizations may cite for not starting a service catalog or portfolio initiative at all can include:

- lack of commitment
- lack of senior management backing
- lack of interest
- lack of understanding
- lack of resources/time/effort
- lack of a basic understanding regarding the service portfolio
- not seen as a risk to the business if not done
- lack of service portfolio capable applications on the market
- costs involved can be high, or perceived to be high
- other business requirements take precedence over the service portfolio

Chapter four provides a framework for creating a service catalog. As part of the "Initiation" phase a feasibility study is to be undertaken which should be used to help understand, amongst others, the reasons for not starting a service catalog or service portfolio initiative mentioned above.

At first glance, creating a service portfolio seems fairly straightforward. Just know what services are coming on line, and what services are active and what services are no longer in use. Put all this information into a document, spreadsheet, database, web page, or repository and there it is: a service portfolio. Well yes, in one sense. As already stated ITIL breaks down the service portfolio into three elements. It makes sense to record all three elements in the same central repository if at all possible. However in reality this may not be possible but is it imperative to **link** together all three elements via a federated approach that links the three elements of the service portfolio together. It is possible to record the service pipeline, service catalogs and retired services in one central repository or via a federated approach, relating service records between different applications. If a single repository is to be used for the entire service portfolio it has to be fit for purpose and fit for use. A single repository may well suit small and medium sized organizations and that is why it has been mentioned here. However the practicalities of finding such a repository may prove difficult. Therefore, the single repository approach may not be realistic for larger organizations due to a number of reasons:

- complexities of services and service mappings
- availability and configurability of service catalog applications software
- lack of integrated systems used in the development and delivery of large scale services
- lack of access to such systems due to purchasing constraints

A process to manage the overall service portfolio will also be required. One key element of the service portfolio management process is the management of the service pipeline which may need to integrate with other processes in the organization, for example financial processes, project management processes and other management functions and any other process that would be involved in bringing services into the service pipeline or retiring them. An output of financial decisions made may be to explore the potential use of a new service in the future. This decision should input into the service portfolio management process and ensure that details about this potential service are added to the service pipeline.

2.6.1 The service portfolio pyramid

This book introduces the service portfolio pyramid represented in figure 2.7. The service portfolio pyramid is a device that helps to identify, by way of a visual aid, the different types of service catalog that can exist in a single diagram. To reiterate, the main focus of this book is placed on the service catalog not the service portfolio, however the service portfolio pyramid is a device that can be used to position the service catalog within the service portfolio, showing the other two elements of the service portfolio which are the service pipeline and the retired services. The concepts within the service portfolio pyramid are not new and should be easily identifiable to those familiar with IT service management. This representation has not been taken directly

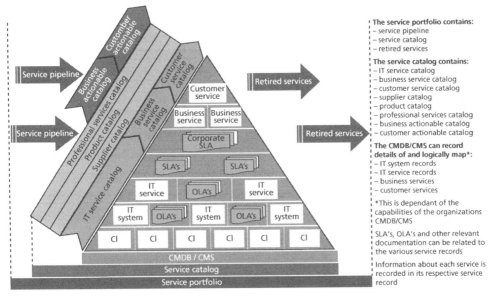

Figure 2.7. The service portfolio pyramid

from any of the ITIL books, but has been developed by the author in order to represent the key elements that make up the service portfolio as described throughout ITIL. It has been kept at a high level to ensure clarity and for ease of use. The service catalogs represented in the service portfolio pyramid will be explained in detail in chapter three and their construction detailed in chapter 4 and 5.

The various elements that go together to make up the service portfolio and were they fit in, are easy to identify in the pyramid. Organizations may find it difficult to implement all elements of the service portfolio at the same time. Taking on too much scope at one time can be ineffective. A gradual approach can help to provide balance and is generally taken. An initial step is generally taken with the need to have a service catalog. Organizations can identify what type of service catalog they need, which will provide value to the business both internally (for example automated service requests reducing labor costs), and externally (for example a customer actionable service catalog that can increase sales and penetrate new markets).

A service catalog can mean different things to different people. Departments working in isolation or silos may not appreciate or even understand the interlink between the different elements that make up the service portfolio pyramid. The different service catalogs can interface with each other, but a unified approach is required to achieve success. It should be clear that no single department or team will be responsible for completing a service portfolio that spans the service portfolio pyramid. If an organization is mature enough to actually have a service portfolio, accountability lies with the service portfolio manager to ensure that the service portfolio exists and is up to date. This does require that the service portfolio manager works closely with the various service catalog managers. If a service portfolio does not exist within the organization, the service catalog manager will retain accountability for managing whatever service catalogs are in place.

The service portfolio pyramid provides a reference to what constitutes the service portfolio.

The service portfolio pyramid is an easy to use representation showing the different service portfolio elements, service catalog types and their associated service records that comprise the service portfolio which helps explain the concept of the service portfolio.

The service portfolio pyramid provides a clear representation of the various catalogs that can exist in any organization:
- *The elements that make up the service portfolio are the service pipeline, service catalog and retired services.*
- *The pyramid represents the different service records that will contain information about each service.*
- *The side of the pyramid represents the different service catalog types that can exist within an organization and maps to their specific service catalog records.*

2.7   The basics - twelve guiding principles

The following section lists twelve guiding principles that apply to the service catalog. These principles are, in the author's view, key aspects that relate to the service catalog. They have not been gathered directly from any framework, standard or reference model. They serve to reference key aspects of the service catalog and to highlight important information at a high level which should be understood and is explained further throughout this book. In essence they have been kept as simplistic in nature as possible to allow the reader to remember key principles that apply to the service catalog. Once these key principles are understood, the task of understanding and creating the relevant service catalog and its various components should become a lot easier.

Guiding principle No. 1	**The service catalog is a subset of the service portfolio of which the service portfolio consists of 3 elements:** • service pipeline • service catalog • retired services

[Handwritten note at top: Service portfolio – may need to have infrastructure be captured 31 Sep from the apps – and infrastructure may evolve from existing to an envisioned future]

Guiding principle No. 2	**There are a number of different service catalog types:** • customer actionable catalog • customer service catalog • business actionable catalog • business service catalog • IT service catalog (consisting of IT services and IT systems) • professional services catalog • product catalog • supplier catalog
Guiding principle No. 3	**At a minimum there must be one overall service catalog covering all service catalog types** • in reality a *federated* approach may be required.
Guiding principle No. 4	**The service catalog consists of a minimum of four service record types:** • customer services • business services • IT services • IT systems
Guiding principle No. 5	**The service catalog should provide a means to link service records together:** • link IT systems to IT services • link IT services to business services • link business services to customer services • (The CMDB/CMS can provide views of the IT service catalog)
Guiding principle No. 6	**A service catalog does not just consist of a list of services:** • service records should contain key information about each service
Guiding principle No. 7	**The service catalog is built on relationships between the different service records:** • without relationships the different service catalog types will remain unconnected; in isolation they will provide limited value • services should be built from a collection of relevant relationships between IT, business and customer service records
Guiding principle No. 8	**Develop the service catalog(s) as early as possible, preferably during the initial design of services:** • it is generally harder to retrospectively understand and map services • coincide with CMDB development especially regarding the IT service catalog • it's better to start late than not at all

[Handwritten note at right margin: get to business add value of IT – link IT to organizations Business strategy]

Guiding principle No. 9	**The service catalog should be scalable:** • the service catalog should be designed to meet the current and known future needs of the organization • the service catalog should also be flexible enough to meet future requirements.

Guiding principle No. 10	**The service catalog should be easy to use:** • the service catalog is made up of a number of different service catalog types each type having different audiences who will have their own specific needs • each service catalog view should be designed so that each audience can use the service catalog view that is relevant to them with ease

[handwritten note: could manage via ABAC]

Guiding principle No. 11	**The journey is not over once the service catalog is completed:** • the service catalog is only as up to date as the last time that it was updated • services and service requirements may change throughout the service lifecycle • changes to services and their respective service record should be controlled under a change management process to ensure controlled change takes place and that service records are kept up to date

Guiding principle No. 12	**The customer trinity:** • the customer is King • the customer has many faces (internal/external) • respect and serve the customer

Table 2.7 Guiding principles

3 The service catalog

The service portfolio pyramid presented in the last chapter clearly shows that there are a number of different service catalog types that can exist within an organization. Some organizations may need to have all these service catalog types in place and operational, while others may not, instead identifying those that will yield the best return to the organization. What these organizations share in common is that they need to be able to identify the different service catalog types and to understand the purpose of each service catalog type in order to effectively decide what service catalog will meet their needs and how to achieve implementing it. This chapter looks at the *what* and chapter four and five look at the *how*.

3.1 Service catalog types

IT systems and IT services are separate service catalog types but together they constitute the IT service catalog. IT personnel may see IT systems as actually IT services. Confusion can be experienced all round when business services are introduced. This is not a failing on anyone's behalf but may be borne from a lack of guidance and information. One reason may be that IT views the services from the technology layer and generally not in the same context as how the user of a business service or the customer of a customer service perceives the service. Regardless it is necessary to clarify these basic definitions throughout the organization to ensure that everybody is talking the same language and that it is clear to all the differences between IT services and IT systems. IT systems and IT services will be discussed in more detail in the following sections.

3.1.1 IT service catalog

Technology enables organizations to work more efficiently and effectively and to deliver more to users and customers quicker, faster and smarter. In order to achieve the required benefits from technology the organization should identify and invest adequately in the technology that is required and discontinue investment in technology that is no longer needed or can be replaced with cheaper alternatives such as investing in virtual technology instead of traditional standalone servers. Cost savings are one of many benefits of taking this approach. Organizations need to understand what technology is required for the core business applications and to ensure that adequate support and maintenance is provided by each supplier/partner. Organizations should identify any gaps in the provision of support in order to address and close out any gaps with the relevant suppliers. Technology decisions should not be based on the latest buzz or hype. They should be based on the best fit that will achieve the organizational requirements that will provide value at an acceptable cost. In the IT service catalog, technology can be broken down into IT systems and IT services. IT systems will be broken down into the CIs that make up that system.

The IT service catalog contains a listing of the **IT systems** and **IT services**, along with information regarding key attributes for the IT systems and IT services contained in their respective service records. The IT service catalog also maintains the relationships between the IT system and IT service records.

IT system:
- is a grouping of CIs that make up an end-to-end IT solution, for example an authentication system or a storage system.
- provides a capability to satisfy a need or objective, for example the ability for all staff to store data, for example file storage
- is built from CIs that (should) exist in the CMDB via relationships between those CIs
- is seen from the IT perspective as a collection of IT CIs

IT service:
- is based on one or more IT systems
- is an IT system that can be charged for/outsourced/paid for
- provides the means to deliver a business or a customer service
- is seen from the IT perspective as a collection of IT systems
- charging can be applied to users of the IT service
- maps to IT systems and not to CIs directly

Key points to note are that the IT service catalog:
- contains details of the technical services
- contains the relationships between IT systems and IT services
- contains relationships between, or links to, CIs and IT systems
- generally written and presented in a technical language or view

Note the use of the word IT within the context of ITIL. ITIL is now heavily focused on the lifecycle of *IT services*. However IT services only form one element of the overall service catalog. The various other elements are discussed in the following paragraphs. Also, IT services form only one element of a service when perceived from the perspectives of the business user or the customer. As explained throughout this book, neither of these audiences sees services as pure technical entities.

The term *IT service* is more frequently used than *IT system* even when people are referring to what are in effect IT systems or even low level IT functions. For example, in the IT world the technologists will even refer to specific daemon functions as services in their own right. In reality these daemon services are generally service programs running on operating systems or applications to ensure that certain activities and tasks are carried out.

It is not enough to just list applications within an IT catalog, as does happen, and assume that constitutes the IT service catalog. Applications play a major part in supporting IT functions and business process. However an application cannot exist on its own. Applications rely on IT infrastructure such as connectivity, storage and security to name just a few. If the application provides functionality that is used by the business, it should be placed in the business service catalog with an appropriate business service record that is linked back to the IT services and IT systems that are required in order for it to work.

An example of this is a content or document management application that is used by a number of business functions such as HR or finance. Such a system provides functionality that supports these business processes and is seen from the view of the user and not in technical terms. However, IT should map the technical elements of this service within the IT service catalog. The application itself may require an IT service record to record its technical details and information and to relate it to the IT systems e.g. infrastructure that is needed to make it work. The users may refer to the content or document management application by its commercial name which may in effect become the service name, in the language of the users and customers.

3.1.2   Business service catalog

The business service catalog contains a listing of the business services, along with information regarding key attributes for the business services contained in their respective service records. The business service catalog should also contain relationships with the IT service records. This catalog represents the services used by personnel within the organization and should be recorded from their perspective in language and format that they understand. Business services rely on technology so there is a direct relationship between the two. Inadequate technological design, support and maintenance can render the best business service ineffective and inefficient.

Business service:
* supports business processes, for example HR service provided by IT services which are made up of IT systems
* is one or more IT services that enable a business process or function
* are services used by the business to support the business
* charging can be applied to the business service
* is seen from the perspective of the business
* is something that delivers value to the business

Key points to note are that the business service catalog:
* contains details of the business services
* should contain the relationships between IT services and business services
* should be written and presented in a language or view that is understood by the business

A further three additional service catalog types that exist, which are not explicitly stated in ITIL, are listed below. They are the:
* customer service catalog
* business actionable catalog
* customer actionable catalog

It is just as important to know and understand these three additional service catalog types as they have quite an important role to play. These are also represented within the *service portfolio pyramid* from chapter 2.

3.1.3   Customer service catalog

Customer services rely on IT services (technology) and adequate business services. Thus, there is a direct relationship between the IT systems, IT services and business services that enable the customer services. Inadequate technological and business design, support and maintenance can also render the best customer service ineffective and inefficient.

The customer service catalog contains a listing of the customer services along with information regarding key attributes for the customer services contained in their respective service record. The customer service catalog should also contain relationships between the business service records which in turn are related to the IT services. This catalog represents the services used by the organization's customers and should be recorded from their perspective.

Customer service:
- is provided to a customer that allows the customer to interact with the organization
- is seen from the perspective of the customer
- is something that you can sell to a customer
- is something that a customer can buy, is willing to pay for and use
- is something that delivers value to customers

Key points to note are that the customer service catalog:
- contains details of the customer services
- contains services that are used by customers to interact with the organization
- should contain the relationships to business services
- should be written and presented in a language or view that is understood by the customer

Note: the three types of service catalog discussed so far, i.e. the IT, business and customer service catalogs, all contain information regarding their particular services and equally as important, they contain the relationships between their different service records. If done correctly, this can build into an end-to-end service model which maps out all the services used by an organization and their customers. This truly is the endgame but be under no illusion as to the complexities that can be faced with achieving such an end-to-end service mapping for any sizeable organization. An example of an end-to-end service mapping (service catalog schematic) is provided in chapter 5.

There is another type of service catalog called "the actionable service catalog" which can be provided to the business users and customers. It is an actual capability to allow users and customers to interact with the organization and order various services. It is still a catalog but needs to do much more than the other three types of service catalog. The actionable service catalog is in effect a service itself. The two types of actionable service catalogs are covered in the following section.

3.2   The actionable service catalog

The service catalog types discussed in the previous sections do not provide functionality that allows users or customers to order goods and services from. They are static by nature and provide a means to represent service mappings and provide information about each service via service

Actually, I believe all the catalogs belong in the Portfolio

catalog records. The actionable service catalog is an element of the service catalog that is published to users and customers and allows them to order goods and services. This service catalog type is considered dynamic.

Actionable service catalogs can be utilized to enable staff to work more efficiently and effectively and to reduce the cost of supporting them by using IT to automate the delivery of service requests. Customers are presented with more and more online and internet capabilities that allow them to interact with organizations even from the comfort of their armchair, given an ordinary computer and a broadband/dial-up connection.

It is quite common that an organization can have any of the following in which to communicate with and provide products and services to both employees and customers:
• an intranet site (internal website)
• an internet site (external public facing website)
• an extranet site (a combination of the two)

An organization may have an internal service catalog (via an intranet) and an external public service catalog and product catalog (via the internet or extranet). The same principle of a service catalog applies in that either type of service catalog exists to allow an end-user or customers to interact with the organization.

The actionable element of the internal service catalog could simply be an extension of the organizations service management system if it has such capability. If so leveraging this ability can aid in maximizing investment made in the service management system and can also help yield an appropriate return on investment by not having to purchase another system.

This approach can:
• utilize economies of scale (less cost)
• utilize existing assets and infrastructure
• automatically create service request records
• utilize service management systems workflow engine/capabilities

While some service management systems have inbuilt functionality to provide actionable service catalog capabilities, for example APIs (Application Programming Interface) and web page functionality, others do not or are so basic that they are not fit for the purpose of an actionable service catalog. Either way the organization should:
• recognize the importance of understanding what it is they need from the actionable service catalog (the requirements)
• know who is involved (people)
• have clear understanding of what will happen (the process)
• identify the correct technology (products & partners)

It is important to involve a number of users of the actionable service catalogs in the design and testing of the catalogs. Their input is required in developing an actionable service catalog that will be relevant, understood and successful with its users. Users should also be allowed to test the catalog and be part of the User Acceptance Testing (UAT) of the catalog before it is fully published to all. This approach should ensure that a useable and relevant actionable service catalog is provided in a format that is clear, understandable and easy to use. Service catalog design is examined in more detail in chapter 4 and 5.

3.2.1 Public face of the service catalog

The business and customer service catalog provides information about services which is contained in the different service records and also provides a logical representation of the services by the relationships between the service records. The actionable service catalogs allow for users and customers to use specific services that are provided to them in an interface that allows them to order services from. There is another element to the service catalog that will help realize such requirements. Presenting the service catalog in a manner that allows users to interact with, or request some action in regards that service, is in fact providing an actionable service catalog. This type of service catalog can help the organization realize:

- cost savings
- efficiencies
- automation
- improved customer experience
- improved customer service
- breaking into new markets and market spaces

The most basic internal actionable service catalog can be found in organizations that allow users to log service requests via an intranet page. The most general external service catalog can be represented by online stores that allow users to not only by products and services, but that also allow them to manage their own account and specific details about their preferences and to submit queries and problems to a support group.

Typical traits of an actionable service catalog include:
- it should be presented in everyday language that the user understands
- it needs to be easy to navigate for the user to find what it is that they are looking for
- it presents a list of the services that the users understand which are available for them to *order*, for example a new laptop request, the ability for a user to release a blocked email themselves, the ability to book an appointment, et cetera
- it may have the functionality of a shopping cart
- different users can have different levels of access depending on their entitlement to a particular service
- it may also allow the user to see the status of their interaction and any history associated with it, for example is it pending, approved or declined (like the Amazon.com tracking facility)
- it provides management with a view of the services being used, who ordered the services and the number people using particular services

The actionable service catalog is an interface presented to users and customers for them to *order* particular services that relate to them. The services are presented to the user or customer in a manner that they can understand and relate to.

The basics of an actionable service catalog are outlined in figure 3.1.

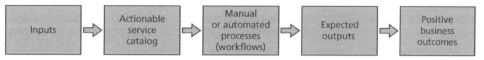

Figure 3.1 Basics of an actionable service catalog

It is important to ensure that expected output and positive business outcomes are achieved. The actionable service catalog is capable of realizing these if it has been set up correctly and if it fulfills users and customers needs and wants. Not only does the technology have to be set up correctly but it must support the underlying processes and sub-processes that are needed. Both must co-exist and work together if expected outputs and positive outcomes are to be achieved.

3.2.2 Business actionable catalog

The business actionable catalog is the service catalog *service* that allows the organizations users (staff) to interact with the organization in relation to ordering services that are made available to them. The business actionable catalog is an interface that provides a list of additional services that the organizations users can request, similar to a shopping list, which can then be logged, processed, managed, fulfilled and completed. The business service catalog provides the means to order these additional services, and it is the request fulfillment process that manages the completion of these service requests. Actionable service catalogs tend to utilize high standards of presentation along with ease of use, although standards may decrease with the business service catalog as it is not public facing. Strive to ensure that this does not happen as the organizations employees are, after all, customer of IT.

At a basic level the organizations staff could be offered the facility to log online requests to the service desk and order available goods and services via a website. The user could also have the ability to manage their preference options for the website. A simple website offering such basic functionality could be built around the organizations existing service management system and could provide a basic actionable service catalog. The ability to integrate the existing service management system with the actionable service catalog will help streamline the provision of services and the fulfillment of requests. The service request may be completed automatically using automated workflow from within the service management system or at a minimum logged automatically within the service management system and assigned to the appropriate group for completion.

Typical traits of a business actionable catalog include:
* it is made available to employees of the organization
* it is generally provided through the organizations internal web presence (intranet)
* it is not generally accessible via the public domain (internet) but can be made available via VPN (Virtual Private Networks)
* it provides access to services that support and allow users carry out their duties
* it uses workflow to provision requests quicker and reduce time lost and the costs associated with manually completing service requests

Key points to note are that the business actionable catalog:
- should be written and presented in a language or view that is understood by the user
- provides an interface or ability for a user to use services provided internally by the business
- provides services that facilitate the organization in achieving its objectives

3.2.3 Customer actionable catalog

The customer actionable catalog is the service catalog *service* that allows the organizations **customers** to interact with the organization and allows them to use or consume services that are made available to them. Similar to the business actionable catalog, the customer actionable catalog is an interface that provides a list of additional services that the organizations customers can request, similar to a shopping list, which can then be logged, processed, managed, fulfilled and completed. The customer service catalog provides the means to order these additional services, and it is the request fulfillment process that manages the completion of these service requests.

Typical traits of a customer actionable service catalog are that it:
- is made available to customers of the organization
- is generally provided through the organizations external web presence (internet)
- is accessible via the public domain (internet)
- provides customers with access to services offered by the organization
- generally offers services that facilitates customers in ordering products and services from the organization
- utilizes high standards of presentation along with ease of use for the customer

Key points to note are that the customer actionable catalog:
- is the service catalog *service* that allows customers to interact with the organization
- should be written and presented in a language or view that is understood by the customer
- provides services that facilitate customers to interact with the organization
- may be provided with a product catalog as additional value-add services

There are an additional three catalogs that may need to be created. None of these appears in the ITIL glossary (at the time of printing) but do have relevance and merit in their own right. These are not discussed in detail throughout this book but are referenced in the *service portfolio pyramid* and do serve very useful functions:
- product catalog
- supplier catalog
- professional services/auxiliary services catalog

3.2.4 Product catalog

A product catalog is at its simplest, a catalog of product listings. Traditionally product catalogs were paper based detailing products available from an organization. More advanced product catalogs can be produced and many are now available online via the internet. Many of these are now utilizing newer technologies such as web 2.0 and advances in specific applications and languages that help render specific content to specific markets and customers. A product catalog can provide additional information such as:
- product description
- product availability

- product price
- product reviews
- product comparisons

It is quite common to have a product catalog and an actionable catalog presented together within the same interface. The product catalog provides the means to find and view information about products that are available to users and customers. The actionable service catalog provides the ability and interface to order these products and to use any other services that are provided to users and customers. Table 3.1 represents some differences between products being offered internally within an organization to its users or externally to the organizations customers. The main difference is that the customer has ultimate control over what they want (as long as it is within their means and is available) but the end-user within the organization may be restricted to making choices for products due to a limited selection available for financial reasons.

Internal services (organization user)	External services (customer)
Limited selection to choose from, for example specific models.	As wide a model selection as the organization can offer.
Limited configurations, for example only specific peripherals.	As wide a configuration selection as the organization can offer.
Generally requires internal approval before being purchased, for example line management/procurement (internal order process).	Requires payment credentials to be approved generally through a 3rd party service, for example credit card services.
Delivery may be to a central department, for example service desk/line manager.	Delivery as per customer's instructions.
Financial constrains such as a maximum budget to spend during a certain period may be exceeded thus preventing any additional purchasing to take place.	Adequate supplies need to be maintained or are capable of being sourced on demand.

Table 3.1 Differences between products being offered internally or externally

Services

The service offered depends on whether it is offered to the organizations users or their customers, each having different traits and elements to the services.

HR employee on-boarding and off-boarding, also known as the new-hires and leavers process is a specific service that can be initiated or requested from the actionable service catalog. Typically this could include any of the following activities:

- request new accounts, for example directory services account
- email account & setup
- new computer
- security access card
- new phone (desk, cell)

However HR employee on-boarding may not be typical of services that an organization would provide to their customers. Instead services such as setting an online account or viewing and tracking orders can be provided. Regardless of whether these services apply internally or externally their activities are associated with request fulfillment which is now recognized in ITIL as its own distinct process.

Paper based catalogs - really?

An example of a paper based product catalog is a catalog of toys that is produced and distributed by a toy store retailer. They will most likely produce and distribute a printed catalog on a regular basis. Like any decent product catalog it shows the customer what the store has to sell. It also provides the customer with information on store opening times, store locations, store phone numbers, and prices. This is an example of a traditional paper based product catalog. The retailer could provide the exact same content through its website which would be the electronic version of the paper based product catalog. A mail order catalog is an example of a product catalog that allows the customer to purchase products and potentially services from an organization. In the mail order catalog example the product catalog has become an actionable catalog as it allows the customer to order products and potentially services from the organization. Equally, the retailer could provide the exact same content through its website which would be the electronic version of the paper based actionable catalog.

These paper based product catalogs still have a place in today's society. Using paper based catalogs is the way that some organizations, particularly retailers, have "interacted" with customers in the past. Not every customer will have a PC but most people have a mailbox and an address. While customers may have a PC and access to the internet some may neither trust online shopping to be safe and secure nor be comfortable with using, nor know how to use, online shopping sites. Organizations have recognized this and some will continue to send out their product catalogs as well as continue to offer goods and service via their website. Some organizations strategy may just focus exclusively on web content as a route to market, some stick to paper based catalogs and others may use a blend of both.

3.2.5 Supplier catalog

The supplier catalog can be used to record information about the suppliers that provide services, systems and support to the organization. It could also be used to record services that your organization provides to other organizations. If using this type of catalog be sure to identify clearly which type it is. If it is to include both "service supplied to …" and "services supplied by …" type services be sure to categorize these clearly. If using this type of catalog it would be beneficial to link the service records from the technical and business catalogs to the service records contained in the supplier catalog. That way the suppliers of each service are clearly identifiable, and information about each supplier including contact details and agreed service levels are easily assessable.

Another approach to take is to record supplier details directly within the relevant service catalog service records. Details of the service supplier such as *supplier name, support responsibilities* and *contact details,* to name but a few, can be recorded as attributes of the service records. This approach allows the organization to utilize current service catalog technology to provide a supplier catalog without the need for further investment in additional products or applications and integrates with the current service catalog types in place.

ITIL references a supplier and contracts database (SDC) within the Service Design book. The scope of this type of database and its function is outside of the scope of this book but it is mentioned here to allow the reader to refer to ITIL for further information if required.

3.2.6 Professional services catalog

The professional services catalog is where details of specific services that can be provided by the organization or within the organization are recorded. These professional services are generally services provided by people as opposed to applications. Some professional services utilize internal staff, some external personnel and other a mixture of both. The professional services catalog is an optional catalog as not every organization will have the need for one. Although these services may be provided exclusively by IT their presentation to the organization should not be through a technical catalog or described in technical language (as is the case for the IT service catalog). It is realistic to record information about the professional services within the business service catalog and classify them as professional services for clarity. The professional services catalog can utilize business service records to record information about these services. In addition, professional services can be offered to the business or customers via an actionable service catalog from which they can actually order these services. To recap, the information about professional services can be recorded within the business service catalog and users and customers can order these services via an actionable service catalog. A professional services catalog can provide additional information such as:

- services that can be provided by resources within IT, or by other parts of the organization
- services that facilitate IT services & business systems, for example business analysis, architecture & design and project management
- costs and prices associated with using the professional services
- details of how to use the service
- details on how to order these services

Examples of professional services include:
- technical consulting
- internal audit preparation
- testing
- architecture and design
- application development

It is reasonable for a department or business unit to cross charge another department or business unit for using a particular professional service, especially if charging has been established within the organization.

It is possible to come up with additional service types. However, plan to start with the service types that have been discussed within this chapter initially as there is a good chance of fitting many of the services found in organizations under one of these service type categories. Remember to:
- start with the minimum number of service types
- see how they fit within the mappings of existing services
- identify any additional service type categories (only those that are needed)
- keep it manageable

The different service catalog types, with the possible exception of the actionable service catalog, can be conceivably stored in one repository. In ITIL terms this single repository could conceivably be the CMS but it does not have to be. Regardless of the medium used, service records should be categorized for identification purposes, which can be achieved quite easily, and related to each other. If not, the service records can be interlinked between different repositories and categorized appropriately. The organizations services are represented by the service records and the relationships that exist between the service records. That is why they could exist within a CMDB, providing it has the capability to relate service records to one another. It is also important to be able to measure delivery of service against agreed levels of service as defined in service level targets.

Actionable service catalogs will require specific functionality and may need specialist applications and functionality. They can be unique in their overall design and content but at the same time use familiar elements such as shopping carts, personalized recommendations and payment options and facilities. There are a number of specialist applications now available that provide actionable service catalog functionality for both internal and external use. Careful consideration must be made if choosing to purchase or even build an actionable service catalog. Identify and understand the current requirements but equally try as much as possible to plan now for future user and development requirements.

4 Framework for creating a service catalog

This chapter will focus on approaches that can be used in order to create a service catalog be it a technical, business, supplier catalog or an actionable service catalog. These approaches can be applied to large or small service catalog initiatives. The concepts described cover the common areas that must be focused on in order to achieve a service catalog that is fit for purpose and fit for use which delivers value back to the organization by facilitating desired outcomes.

4.1 Introduction

Chapter one contained the scenario of the manager delegating out the task of creating the service catalog. Seems simple enough from the outset but this is a task that can quickly become very daunting. The task of delivering a service catalog is not a menial one. Even if the decision has been made that the service catalog will be no more that a series of documents ownership needs to be assigned from the onset to ensure that the tasks and activities required to produce the documents are identified, understood and carried out. Somebody needs to be accountable for the final product i.e. the service catalog and to ensure that requirements have been correctly translated into the design and build stages and correctly tested, deployed and published.

Should every service catalog initiative begin with a project? Every service catalog initiative should be well managed, address the requirements, tested and authorized before being implemented and published. Depending on the size and scale of the service catalog initiative different approaches to the management of the development and delivery of the service catalog can be taken. A formalized and structured project management approach e.g. PMI or PRINCE2 is certainly required when undertaking medium and large scale service catalog implementations to ensure that they are delivered on time, within cost and to specification. Such a project could include implementing a global business actionable catalog for a large organization or developing a technical service catalog within the existing CMDB for a medium to large sized organization.

Regardless of their size, small, medium and large organizations may not have the resources, time or experience to manage projects in a formal structured manner. Smaller implementations may not require the full rigor of formalized project management principles but do need to cover a number of areas in order to be successful. The information contained within this chapter is not a substitute for project management at any level but highlights a number of key areas that need to be considered, planned and implemented in order to deliver a successful service catalog. This section introduces a framework that can be used by organizations of any size.

The framework recommends that a project manager is appointed. If the organization is unable to allocate a full time project manager, it may be possible to utilize a dedicated project manager on a part time basis. If the organization cannot appoint either a full time or a part time project manager someone must be appointed that will have overall responsibility for the delivery of the service catalog initiative. By not appointing an experienced project manager it can lead to sub optimal results especially if the appointed person is inexperienced, under-resourced or overworked or is uncommitted to achieving the desired results.

4.2   Framework overview

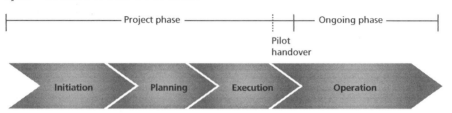

Figure 4.1 Framework stages for creating a service catalog

The framework contains two main phases consisting of the project phase and the ongoing phase. Within these two phases there are four stages, three of which fall under the project phase and one that falls under the ongoing phase. The framework stages for creating a service catalog are listed below and described in detail in the following sections. These framework stages can also be considered high level tasks within a project Work Breakdown Structure (WBS) when planning the service catalog initiative or project. This framework is not a substitute for formal project management principles but provides, at a high level, areas that should be included within the service catalog project.

Initiation
- develop a business case
- undertake a feasibility study
- establish the project charter   — *what should be in the project charter*
- appoint the project team

Planning
- create project plan   — *does QED have?*
- create financial plan
- create risk plan   — *Any risks we are concerned w/?*
- create requirements specification   — *Feature list*
- create acceptance criteria
- create procurement plan

Execution
- design
- build   *| configure / populate*
- test   *(what does one test for something like this?)*
- evaluation
- approve
- deploy / publish

Service Strategy)

*Service Design + Transition *

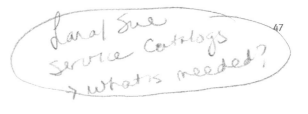

Operations

- pilot
- handover
- steady State
- continual service improvement
- audit and verification

Alvin: Any NGA experience?

4.3 Initiation

4.3.1 Develop a business case

A business case is a document that is used to provide necessary information to the organization on whether or not the service catalog project is worth the investment that will be required. The business case document should include details about the business need for the service catalog and a cost-benefit analysis which will be used as a basis to justify the service catalog project. Benefits of the service catalog, for each of the service catalog types, which can be used in the business case include:

Technical service catalog

- facilitates business impact assessments
- identifies opportunities for the consolidation of IT infrastructure and architecture thus reducing IT service costs
- provides support teams with a complete view of the IT infrastructure that is needed for the provision of services, on a service by service basis thus aiding troubleshooting and incident restoration
- provides application and technical management with information that aids in the re-design of existing services and the design of new services
- can capitalize on investments made in the CMS, thus increasing the ROI of the CMS

Business and customer service catalogs

- provides a means to recover costs and charge users and customers fairly and in an equitable manner
- IT can demonstrate the value it provides to the organization by identifying the business services that rely on IT
- IT can demonstrate its strategic importance to the organization
- the organization can identify with, and understand, what it is that IT does
- improve the relationship between IT, the organization and the users of services
- creates a service, not product, culture
- service users and customers can identify the services that they use

Actionable service catalog

- reduce manual effort and thus costs via workflow management
- empower users and customers to use "self-help" and "self-serve" services
- standardizes services offered to users and customers
- opens routes to new and existing markets from which to provide goods and services to users and customers
- consolidates the provision and delivery of services

Supplier catalog
- identifies opportunities for the consolidation of IT infrastructure and infrastructure providers
- easy access to supplier information, details, and contracts
- provides a foundation for managing suppliers

Product
- provides users and customers with details of available products
- provides opportunities for the consolidation products
- provides a foundation for products offered through the actionable service catalog

Professional
- identifies professional services that are provided internal or even external to the organization
- from an IT point of view, identifies services that can provide added value to the organization for which IT can also charge for
- in conjunction with the other service catalogs, will facilitate the identification of new services that could be needed and potentially provided

All service catalogs
- services are clearly defined and managed
- provides reliable and accurate information about all services
- identify inefficient, ineffective and costly services that do not have any strategic importance
- allow the relocation of resources to critical services
- provide a consistent, repeatable framework and process for the identification, recording and management of all services
- give service providers, even those internal to the organization e.g. IT with a competitive advantage as they can easily articulate their services and service value to users and customers

4.3.2 Undertake a feasibility study

Once the business case has been approved, initial resources and funding can be provided to undertake the feasibility of producing the service catalog. This is critical for medium and large scale service catalog projects especially where a service catalog application is required. Smaller service catalog projects should still consider the questions below; even if the service catalog is to be produced in document or spreadsheet format as they are still applicable.

Questions to be asked at the feasibility stage include:
- How does an organization go about developing a service catalog?
- What is a service catalog, and where do they sit within the service portfolio?
- Which service catalog types are needed?
- Will deliverables meet expectations (i.e. requirements)?
- What is the starting point?
- How will we know when the service catalog is complete?
- How do we maintain the service catalog throughout its life time in order to keep it complete, accurate and up to date?
- What does the organization actually know about service catalogs?
- What does the organization not know about service catalogs?
- How will it be delivered?

- How much will it cost (estimated vs. actual)?
- Is there management backing and sponsorship and at what management level?
- Is there funding available?
- Is there willingness within the organization to help?
- When is the best time for the organization to do this?
- What value does the organization put on having a service catalog?
- What value will be provided back to the organization if a service catalog is created?

The information contained throughout this book will help in completing the feasibility study and in addressing many of these questions. Table 4.1 is a very basic checklist that provides a quick, high level snapshot of some of the more basic challenges that the organization may face and that need to be taken into consideration. Each consideration needs to be analyzed carefully. This table serves to highlight some of the high-level considerations that should be explored. Where shortcomings have been identified further in-depth analysis should be undertaken to understand the reasons why, and causes of, these shortcomings. Remediation plans need to be considered that will address the issues and concerns raised.

Pre-Checklist: Tick each consideration as appropriate. *— good checklist*

Consideration	High	Medium	Low	None
Service catalog knowledge and understanding				
Finance (setup/ongoing costs)				
Management backing				
Enthusiasm/motivation				
Organizations ability to change				
Organizations need to change				
Resistance to change				
Pressure to change				
There is a clear and shared vision				
Urgency				
Risk of not implementing				
Impact of not implementing				
Return on investment				

Table 4.1 Basic high level feasibility checklist

Benefits, constraints and dependencies

The following table looks at additional benefits, constraints and various dependencies that should also be considered.

Service Catalog Type	Benefits	Constraints	Dependencies
Business & customer actionable catalog	Customer services can be delivered quicker, better, smarted and faster.	Costs.	Understanding the needs of the users and customers of the actionable service catalog.
		Geographical reach.	
		Language.	
		Customer culture.	
	New markets can be accessed easier.	Finding technology that is fit for purpose and fit for use.	
Customer service catalog	Provides information that can be used at a strategic level to understand what services customers are using and not using.	Services may be seen internally from an IT perspective.	Requires the ability and knowledge to understand the relationship between the customer services, business services and the enabling IT services.
	Provides an understanding of what existing service platforms can be utilized to reduce the cost of new services.	Business management may not understand how IT is involved in provision and support of customer services.	Requires business analyses with technical acumen to fully understand the relationships.
Business service catalog	Maps out the services as perceived by the users of the service.	Different users of the same business service may perceive it differently from one another. This may make the service mapping or service representation more difficult.	Requires the ability and knowledge to understand the relationship between the business services and the enabling IT services.
	Services are recorded and presented in non-technical language.		
	SLAs can be clearly referenced to the relevant service.	Large organizations may have a larger number of business services.	
IT service catalog	IT departments should have at least an understanding of IT systems thus should be able to draw on their knowledge to input into the IT service catalog.	IT systems may not be mapped to a sufficient level of detail.	Requires a complete understanding of how IT systems are constructed.
	OLAs can be clearly references to the relevant service.	Projects to introduce new systems may not have focused on handing over adequate details about services introduced.	Requires an understanding of what IT systems make up what IT services.
	Organizations are likely to have information about their CIs thus reducing the effort required in identifying, validating and recording CIs.	Significant effort is required if there is an immature or non-existent CMDB in place.	Requires mature understanding of CIs to be effective.
	May utilize CMDB relationship mapping capabilities.	Existing CI relationships may be incorrect, out of date or non-existent.	CI relationships need to be understood/developed and mapped.

Table 4.2 Various benefits, constraints and dependencies that should be considered

A critical question that has to be asked is: *"When **should** an organization develop the service catalog?"* Failing to develop a service catalog as early as possible will lead to an exercise in retrospectively identifying, understand and mapping the services used throughout the organization. This can prove difficult for a number of reasons including lost knowledge and the lack of documentation. The people who built the services may no longer be available and services may not have been documented in enough detail or at all.

The best time for an organization to actually develop a service catalog is as early as they possibly can. However the reality is that many organizations have not done so. Equally organizations may have developed the different types of service catalogs in isolation and may not have linked them together or may not have the ability, expertise or knowledge to make the connection. This is not a failing on the organizations part as such. It is to be expected that organizations may focus initially on their core objectives and activities that lead the organization to its success e.g. to sell DVDs online, to build renewable energy solutions, to sell hamburgers. A common trait is that organizations, and in particular start up organizations, are less likely to be focused on the creation of service catalogs and more focused on just getting business processes and operational activities done. By the time they are in full operation mode and realize that that there is benefit in creating a service catalog, it is a more difficult, time consuming and expensive retrospective exercise.

4.3.3 Establish project charter

The project charter is a document that is used to formally authorize the service catalog project and will include the documentation of the initial requirements. Key inputs into the project charter are the business case and the feasibility study. The approval of the project charter is the formal recognition of the service catalog project initiation. It is during the development of the project charter that the project manager should be appointed who should also be involved in the final project charter document. The project charter gives the project manager authority to start appointing resources, initially the project team, to project activities.

4.3.4 Appoint project team

Confirm the resources that will be needed to complete the project activities and then obtain them. The project team may consist of a mix of the organizations staff and external personnel, e.g. contractors or consultants, especially if during the design stage the need to purchase a service catalog application is identified. The resources that will be needed to define both the definition of services and the logical build of the services should be identified at this stage, as well, as their input and involvement in the overall project is critical. After all, if the services cannot be defined or they cannot be logically mapped out there may be little value provided from the IT and business service catalog.

4.4 Planning

4.4.1 Create project plan

The project plan defines how the project will be executed, monitored, controlled and finally closed. The content of the project plan will vary depending on the size and complexity of the service catalog project and should include three key elements which will be used as the project baselines. These key elements are listed in table 4.3 and will allow for the service catalog project to be executed, measured, monitored and controlled. When the requirements have been identified and documented (section 4.4.4) the Work Breakdown Structure (WBS) can be completed. Include in the project plan a pilot phase as discussed in section 4.6.1 Pilot.

Key element/ Baseline	Benefit	Document
Scope baseline	To prevent scope creep and ensure project boundaries are set.	Scope document.
Cost baseline	To manage cost and reduce the likelihood of cost overruns.	Budgets.
Schedule baseline	To manage resources and reduce the chance of time overruns.	Work Breakdown Structure (WBS).

Table 4.3 Key elements

4.4.2　Create financial plan

To ensure that the service catalog project is delivered within the expected and approved budget the following need to be taken onto consideration:

Financial considerations	Details
Estimate costs	The cost of completing the service catalog project and the project activities must be estimated. The project plan, schedule baseline and WBS should all be used to estimate the approximate costs that will be involved in the service catalog project. The following list contains a number of basic costs that need to be estimated: • service catalog application costs • actionable service catalog application costs • licensing costs (for new or existing applications) • design / build / test costs • consultancy fees • resources (salaries and contractor/consultancy fees) • expenses • training costs • pilot costs • contingency (emergency funds) The costs involved in the operation of the service catalog are not project costs but it is advisable to identify such costs at this early stage so that the organization can estimate how much it is likely to cost to operate the service catalog year on year.
Determine budget	The project budget is comprised of the authorized funds that are made available to execute the project. The overall cost estimates for the service catalog project are required before the actual budget can be finalized and agreed. The budget then becomes the project cost baseline.
Control costs	The service catalog project should be delivered on time and within budget. Management of costs against the cost baseline throughout the project is vital if this is to be achieved. Any changes in costs or the requirement for additional funds must be carefully managed and evaluated against the value that will be achieved or lost, relative to the increase or decrease in costs.

Table 4.4 Financial considerations

4.4.3 Create risk plan

Risks are uncertain conditions that may occur in the future and if so will have an effect on project activities and potentially the quality of the service catalog. At a minimum, create a risk register that will record all known risks identified at the start of the project and the risks that are identified throughout the life of the project. Risks may have a negative effect on the time, quality, cost, utility and warranty factors which in turn affect the ultimate delivery of the service catalog.

4.4.4 Create requirements specification

Service catalog requirements will differ depending on which of the different service catalog types are to be delivered. Actionable service catalogs are different in nature to the business or IT service catalog. They can also have different stakeholders, users and customers both internal and external to the organization. The stakeholder, end user and customer representatives need to be involved in the development of the requirements specification if the service catalog is to deliver value to the organization and facilitate desired outcomes.

If different service catalog types are being delivered under a single project it is advisable to separate the different service catalog types into separate deliverables or project streams and to define specific requirements for each service catalog type / project stream. The project charter contains initial high level requirements and therefore the project charter will be a direct input into the requirements specification stage. The identified requirements will form the basis for creating the project Work Breakdown Structure (WBS) which is used to manage project activities, time and resources.

Different techniques can be used to identify and quantify the needs of stakeholders, users and customers and their expectations around what will be achieved with the service catalog which can be analyzed and documented as specific requirements. These techniques include the following which are elaborated further within the design section:

- interviews
- workshops
- questionnaires
- surveys
- observations

Probing questions can be used to help quantify the exact needs of the stakeholders and users of the service catalog. These include:

- **T**ell me … what services, applications or systems you use?
- **E**xplain to me … how these technical components connect together?
- **D**escribe to me … the differences stages in ordering and approving a laptop.

How many service catalogs?

This is an important question and needs to be asked right from the start. It directly relates to the requirements of the organization, its users and their customers. Failing to understand how many catalog types are required may ultimately lead to the service catalog initiative failing to deliver. An organization may require an IT service catalog, a supplier catalog, a business services catalog and an actionable customer catalog but may only purchase an application capable of providing the actionable service catalog element. Those that require the IT service catalog, the supplier catalog and the business services catalog will not have their requirements met meaning that they will be less than satisfied with the outcome.

The following question has been taken from the online USMBOK knowledge base.

Question:
Can a service organization have more than one service catalog?

Answer:
Yes. There is no best practice based ruling on whether a service organization can or should have one or more service catalogs. The primary consideration is the ability of the service organization to present their products and service offerings to each customer constituency, or prospective customer, in terms understood by that audience.

This means that one physical catalog can present multiple views to different audiences (virtual catalogs). It also means that multiple discrete and physically separate service catalogs can be presented as part of a "federated" service catalog system.

The overriding considerations are:
*   presenting service offerings in language and terms understood by the target audience
*   enabling a service model and service request system aligned with the needs of the audience
*   supporting a service organization need to present different service combinations to specific audiences
*   supporting a security related need to segregate specific service offerings and service models

Conclusion:
There is no hard and fast rule for how many service catalogs an organization should have, or must have, except to say it should have ONE.

As echoed in the above reference from USMBOK there needs to be at least one ultimate service catalog repository that has the ability to record information about each service type, link the different service record types together and provide actionable service catalog capabilities. If not, multiple repositories can exist for each service catalog type but there must be a unified way in which all the service record types can be linked together. These can, in theory, exist within a single repository, but more than likely they are to be found in multiple repositories.

4.4.5 Create acceptance criteria

It is important in the early stages of the project to identify the acceptance criteria and the critical success factors. The acceptance criteria are the essential conditions, including performance requirements, which must be acceptable to the stakeholders, users and customers of the service catalog before the service catalog project deliverables are accepted. Acceptance criteria need to be identified in terms of the stakeholder, user and customer representatives and should relate to the utility and warranty of the service catalog.

High level acceptance criteria specific to the service catalog which need to be reviewed with they stakeholder, user and customer representatives include the following:

- delivery dates
- functionality
- appearance
- performance
- capacity
- availability
- reliability
- cost - development and operational
- security
- ease of use / automation

The review should quantify these in terms of what the stakeholders and end-user representatives see as acceptable.

4.4.6 Create procurement plan

The procurement plan describes how the procurement process will be managed. Organizations that have adequate procurement processes in place can use these to manage the procurement of the service catalog applications, resources and consultancy that will be required. Organizations with formally established project management practices may have specialized procurement plan processes and templates which can be used. Organizations without either should look to identify how the procurement process will be managed.

4.5 Execution

4.5.1 Design

During the design stage the definition and construct of services need to be defined. Only after this activity is complete should the organization identify if specific service catalog applications are needed; this especially applies for the actionable service catalogs. Suppliers of resources, services, other applications, interfaces and IT infrastructure may also be required and may need to be formally engaged through a tendering process. Activities will include:

- issue request for information (RFI)
- issue request for proposal (RFP)
- select supplier and negotiate terms, conditions and deliverables
- supplier contract

Organizations that undertake these **application sourcing** activities during the planning stage run the risk of acquiring tools and technology that might not actually provide the necessary functionality and capabilities that are required to provide expected and needed user and customer requirements, therefore devaluing the investment made and the actual value of the service catalog. In other words the Return on Investment (ROI) and the Value of Investment (VOI) can, and most likely will, be significantly reduced.

Additional information on the designing of the different service catalog types is provided in sections 5.3 to 5.7.

4.5.2 Build

The service catalog should be built to the design specification and requirements. Any changes that are needed during the build stage should be properly controlled and managed to ensure that the key stakeholders are adequately informed, understand the risks involved and are willing to accept, or challenge any changes to the original requirements and design specification. Failure to properly manage any deviations, no matter how small, may result in stakeholder, user and customer dissatisfaction and additional time, resources and costs in trying to rectify the situation. It is better to work to the specification and deal with any required deviations under change control ensuring that the key stakeholders accept and approve any changes.

Additional information on the building of the different service catalog types is provided in sections 5.3 to 5.7.

4.5.3 Test

The testing stage of any development is very important. It is the stage that actually checks and validates that the designs that have been built actually work and work as required based on the original designs and requirement specifications. Bugs and errors are detected, analyzed, reviewed and removed to ensure that a stable service catalog is provided. Different levels of testing exist including functional testing and user acceptance testing (UAT).

Additional information on the testing of the different service catalog types is provided in sections 5.3 to 5.7.

4.5.4 Evaluation

ITIL includes a process within Service Transition called Evaluation, figure 4.2. The evaluation process is pertinent when implementing a service catalog. Evaluation is a generic process that allows for a formal evaluation of the service catalog in order to consider whether the performance of the service catalog is acceptable, if it delivers value for money and whether it will be approved for deployment, accepted into use and paid for. The actual performance of the service catalog is assessed against its predicted performance and any deviations between the two are understood and managed. Basically, evaluation is a measure of whether the service catalog will be fit for purpose and fit for use.

Basic inputs into the evaluation process include the documents from the planning stage in particular the requirements specification, the acceptance criteria and critical success factors. These documents will help to evaluate if the service catalog that has been produced will deliver the predicted performance, that it is still relevant and that it will provide value for money.

In addition, consideration must be given to any changes in requirements and CSF's that have occurred during the design, build and test stages of the service catalog especially if a long period of time has elapsed between the original requirements specification and the design, build and testing of the service catalog.

ITIL provides additional details regarding the evaluation process within the Service Transition lifecycle book.

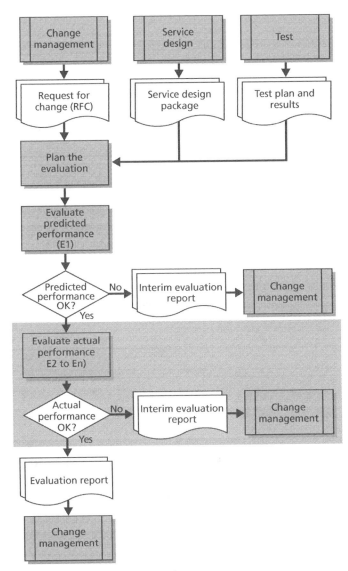

Figure 4.2 Evaluation process (Source OGC)

4.5.5 Approve

The decision to approve the deployment of the service catalog to the live or production environment should be controlled via the change management process and the appropriate Change Advisory Board (CAB). The output of the evaluation process is an evaluation report which is used as an input within the change management process and is an important document to review when deciding if the service catalog is to be deployed. If the evaluation process has identified that the service catalog will not deliver the expected value to the organization, that it is not fit for purpose and fit for use, that what has been designed, built and tested does not meet requirements the decision should be not to deploy until these considerations are met.

4.5.6 Deploy or publish

If the evaluation process has deemed that the service catalog meets the requirements and that it will provide value and if the appropriate request for change (RFC) has been approved, the service catalog can be deployed to the live or production environment. If the service catalog has been produced in document format e.g. word documents or spreadsheets, then these can now be published and made available. Equally, if the service catalog has been built within a specific CMDB, as part of the CMS or has been built within a specific service catalog application, the configuration changes necessary to implement these can now be deployed to the live environment. These can also be published and made available. ITIL handles the release of services under the *release and deployment* process within the service transition lifecycle which can provide more in depth information on this stage including rollout options e.g. big bang versus phased, push and pull and automation versus manual. The roll out option to choose is dependent on the scale of the service catalog that is being released. Once deployed there should be a formal acknowledgement or communication that the service catalog is now deployed and in effect published.

4.6 Operations

4.6.1 Pilot

Deploying and publishing the service catalog to the live or production environment should not be considered the final activities from the project and development team. As with any release there should be an agreed period of time that allows sufficient elements of the project team to remain involved. Some organizations refer to this as the pilot or warranty[9] stage. Pilot allows for a greater chance of being successful with a service catalog initiative or project as a good portion of issues, bugs, errors and omissions can be identified by users of the service catalog (or any new deployment) within the first few days or weeks of deployment depending on usage patterns. These can be dealt with and resolved quickly by the project team who will know the service catalog better at this point in time than the supporting operations teams. Also, it is generally more cost effective in the long run to address issues in this manner than allowing them to remain in the service catalog until the operation support teams can resolve them.

It should be agreed at the "create project plan" stage that a pilot should be included as part of the project to ensure that adequate resources and budget are allocated to cover the pilot period. The length of the pilot period should also be agreed by both the project team and the operation support team's management. Some negotiation may be required as the project team may want to have a shorter pilot to reduce overall project costs and operation support teams may request a longer pilot to ensure that as many issues are dealt with by the project team and not handed over to them to resolve as part of ongoing operations.

---

9   Warranty in this case is not to be confused with the definition of utility and warranty.

4.6.2 Handover

When the agreed pilot is finished the service catalog is formally handed over to operations and the project closed. Before the final handover is complete consideration must be given to the following:

- major issues that have been logged are still open and unresolved
- major flaws exist within the service catalog
- a medium or high level of requirements have not been delivered
- all relevant documentation has been provided to the technical and application operations teams
- sufficient support is available for the service catalog be it internal or external support

Failure to adequately address these areas will lead to user dissatisfaction if required information is not assessable and required functionality is not available. The burden will increase for the supporting technical and application support teams who will have to try and deal with these issues as well as normal operations tasks, with limited or no budget available to resolve the issues and flaws and implement missing requirements.

Handover is one of the final tasks of the service catalog project, handing the service catalog and any actionable service catalog systems over to the service catalog manager. Handover should be formally agreed between the project manager, or in the case of small scale implementation, the project lead, the service catalog owner, the supporting technical and application support teams and any stakeholders representing the users and customers of the service catalog.

4.6.3 Steady state

Once a formal handover has been completed the service catalog project will come to an end and the service catalog manager is responsible for the service catalog. Any major changes or upgrades to the service catalog may require an additional project if the work involved is complex or outside the scope and capability of the supporting operation teams. Even minor modifications and updates applied to the service catalog or actionable service catalog need to be controlled under the change management process.

4.6.4 Continual service improvement

Continual service improvement is used to ensure that the service catalog and its supporting processes remain valid, up-to-date, and relevant and are improved over time. ITIL contains a full book dedicated to continual service improvement which can provide information on improvement initiatives. The service catalog manager should create a continual service improvement plan, or log, and record any improvement initiatives that are identified.

Anyone can input into the improvement plan for the service catalog. Improvements to be identified can include those that will address:

- processes - service catalog management and interfacing processes
- service record forms and the attributes contained within the records
- accessibility / inaccessibility of the service catalog and access to actionable service catalogs
- workflow within the actionable service catalog
- bottlenecks
- changing requirements

4.6.5 Audit and verification

See chapter 6.3 "Service catalog audit process" for further details on the auditing and verification of the service catalog.

5 Design and development

This chapter describes the activities that should be performed in order to design and deliver a service catalog. The activities will be explored in detail for each service catalog type.

5.1 Basic activities

The first activity of the execution stage is to design the service catalog. The basic high level requirements of the service catalog type should have been gathered from the planning stage and will be an important input into this stage. During the design stage, the first and most important activity to be undertaken is the requirements activity. This is where the low level requirements for the service catalog are identified, qualified, quantified and agreed with the users and customers that will actually use the service catalog. As there are a number of service catalogs, discussed in chapter 3, and as each different service catalog will have different audiences, there will be different requirements for each service catalog type. Figure 5.1 represents the most basic design activities that should be carried out in order to deliver a service catalog that is fit for purpose, fit for use and will provide value to the organization and the users of the service catalog.

Figure 5.1 Basic activities

These basic activities will be explored in more detail through the following sections in regards to the following service catalog types:
- IT service catalog
- business service catalog
- customer service catalog
- actionable service catalog

5.2 Service catalog schematic

The schematic in figure 5.2 extends the service portfolio pyramid introduced in chapter 2 and shows the relationships between the different service catalogs types. The service catalog schematic also forms the foundation from which to start the service modeling activity from. Understanding how all the different services relate to each other is a very important modeling requirement as there is a clear hierarchy between these services. Customer and business services cannot exist on their own as they are provided by IT capabilities i.e. IT systems and services. In the diagram the different catalogs are colored the same as their respective service catalog records and the service types that exist within the service catalog. Relationships between the different service catalog types are represented with the blue lines. The diagram clearly shows the actual service type which is represented by the appropriate service catalog record which is contained within a specific service catalog. It is possible that applications that provide CMDB functionality could provide most of the service catalog functionality, with a possible exception for the actionable service catalogs. Regardless, in the ITIL world, the service catalog is an element of the Information Integration Layer of the CMS and therefore all the service catalog types will fall into this layer of the CMS.

Figure 5.2 also highlights a basic mapping structure between each of the different service types. This mapping structure is concerned with relating the service catalog records contained within their respective service catalogs in order to build an end-to-end picture of the entire service. An important point to note about the service record relationships is that there can be multiple relationships between different services especially between the IT systems and IT services therefore requiring their service records to be interrelated also.

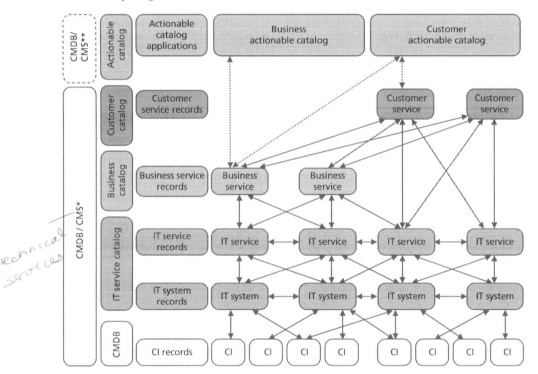

*The CMDB/CMS could be used to store these service records if it can classify the service records appropriately and can create the appropriate relationships between the service records.

**If the CMDB cannot support actionable service catalog capabilities and a specific application is used it will still form part of the Information Integration Layer of the CMS

Figure 5.2 Service catalog schematic

Chapter 2.5 contains details of basic information that should be recorded for these core service catalog records.

Business Impact Assessment

Business Impact Assessment (BIA) provides information that helps establish potential impact and understand the full impact of a loss of partial loss of a service to the organization and customers. BIA aims to identify the most important services from a business perspective, which can then be classified as critical services within their service catalog records. BIA helps to identify the effect that service disruption or the total loss of a service or multiple services may have on the organization as a whole. This includes the effect on customer services which may be revenue affecting, as well as the internal impact to the organization. If the service catalog contains adequate service mappings, relationships and service records it will become an important asset to assist in establishing how service impacts will affect the organization and its customers. The service catalog schematic shows the relationships between each of the service catalog types which will allow for business impacts to be assessed against all the different service catalog types.

5.3 IT service catalog design

The IT service catalog contains information at a technical level. Therefore the IT service catalog will generally be written and presented in technical terms. It can also have a direct link to the CMDB/CMS. Depending on the system it may even be built within the CMDB/CMS. As previously seen, the IT service catalog can contain information regarding:

* IT systems
* IT services

Areas that need careful consideration include:
* CIs that make up IT systems need to exist in the CMDB
* auto-discovery tools can be used to identify CIs but the data needs to be validated and any variance of baseline CI attributes must be identified via change management
* making relationships may be a manual task which increases the administration and upkeep of the service catalog and the possibility of inaccurate relationships
* the scope of IT systems may be vast, especially for larger organizations
* identifying key critical systems and services to be included initially will help focus on the important services first

The IT service catalog is the technical element of the service catalog that will facilitate IT in:
* understanding the IT systems and services that exist
* understanding the relationships and dependencies between the IT systems and IT services
* understanding the impact that IT systems failures will have on IT services
* referencing CI components that make up the IT systems to aid in fault resolution and incident management
* mapping out the IT infrastructure in one central repository
* providing a service map of all IT systems and services which will be linked to their relevant OLA's, SLA's and contracts

Remember that in general neither IT systems nor IT services are understood by users or customers. Any why should they? After all, is it not the responsibility of IT to know and understand the IT systems and services that they provide, support and maintain on behalf of the organization?

5.3.1 Requirements

By now the business requirements for the IT service catalog should be known. Now is the time to identify what information is required which needs to be recorded for IT systems and IT service records. At a minimum the following information should be recorded:

- attributes
- status
- service records
- relationships

Description	Detail
Attributes	• Contains the information recorded about the IT service/IT system. • Workflows (automation) can be triggered from changes in attribute values. • Define attributes that will provide relevant information. • Too many attributes may be difficult to maintain accurately. • Too little may not provide any value. • Each attribute should have an owner who can provide accurate and up to date information for the attribute. • Important attributes should be mandatory. Generally the mandatory requirement is based on the status or other attributes as they change.
Status	• Is an attribute. • Denotes where in the service portfolio lifecycle the service record is. • Should be a mandatory field that needs to be completed.
Service records	• This is the form that contains the information about the IT services and contains a relationship to the operational level agreement for that service. • Also used to contain information about IT systems. • Can be the same form that is used for CIs in the CMDB - but needs to be classified or categorized as a service record.
Relationships	• Links CIs to CIs to form IT systems. • Links IT systems to form IT services. • Should have forward and reverse relationships.

Table 5.1 Information that needs to be recorded

5.3.2 Model

A detailed understanding of the IT systems and services is required in order to be able to properly map these appropriately. This also requires a good understanding of how they all relate to one another. The first steps involved in the modeling of IT systems and services are to understand:

- What IT systems and services exist?
- How the IT systems and services relate to one another?

There are a number of methods that can be used to find out this information, which include:

- interviews / one-on-one sessions
- workshops
- change requests
- knowledge base
- project documentation

Interviews and one-on-one sessions

Interviews and one-on-one-sessions are used as a formalized means to gather information and knowledge. To be successful, the following section lists a number of basic steps that should be followed:

Identify who to interview:
- Technical people, support teams, service desk, project staff.

Identify what information is needed / prepare questions:
The interviews are used to gather the information that is required. Prepare a number of standard questions that are likely to lead to the interviewee providing the necessary information. Open questions can be used to tease out information with such as: what, why, how, describe. Closed questions can be used to gather facts.
- What IT systems and services are in use?
- What are they used for?
- Who typically uses or relies on them?
- How they are connected / related?
- How critical are they to the organization?
- Who is responsible for the service?

Schedule the interview:
- Agree date and time.
- Provide interviewees with a brief agenda.

Conduct interview(s):
- Carry out the interview(s) as per the schedule.

Document findings:
- Confirm understanding of information with the interviewer.
- Summarize the information that has been provided on a per system or service basis.

Workshops

Workshops can be used to facilitate gathering information from a number of different people at one time. The attendees can be coordinated to work together and collectively pool their knowledge and understanding of the IT systems and services. Whiteboard sessions can be used to map out known systems and services quicker than trying to piece all the information together from individual interviews. Technical managers and members of their support teams, project staff and service desk personnel should attend such sessions. Workshops should be structured in order to get the maximum benefit from the time available.

Workshops can also be used to work with service owners and to help them understand their role in the design of a service catalog which supports their needs and can represent the services that they are responsible for. Rigorous engagement with the service owners should be conducted via workshops, communication planning and execution.

Change requests

Change requests should contain a level of technical information regarding the IT components or services that are being changed. By examining such detail from change requests it may be possible to build up a picture of IT infrastructure that is in use and how it all relates to each other. The change manager is also a good source of information as over time they may have built up a good understanding of the IT infrastructure from attending CAB meetings and discussing changes in general. The information found from change requests should also be used in the interviews with technical staff in order to understand how it all fits together in more detail.

Knowledge base and information stores

Some organizations have a formal knowledge base(s) while others do not. Some will have specialist knowledge management applications while others may utilize structures such as basic shared folders to store knowledge and information in the form of documents. Some will have a formalized knowledge management process and other will not. Regardless, the task is to identify the sources of information and knowledge within the organization that may contain relevant information regarding the IT systems and services. This may be challenging especially within an organization that does not formally manage information and knowledge. Key information regarding the relationship between IT systems and services may be found within:

- system schematic diagrams – showing the design of IT systems and services
- network topology diagrams – showing the relationship of IT systems and services
- ad-hoc documents – such as documents created by support teams detailing information about an IT system or service

Technical support teams should be able to provide details on where to locate this information. It is also advisable to sit with the service desk and to go through their information and knowledge stores, which although may be separate to those of the technical support teams, may contain the same, similar or additional information and knowledge.

Project documentation

If projects are used to deliver new IT systems and services within the organization, they can provide a wealth of information and knowledge in the form of initial and final design and build documents. The documentation may only be as up to date as the time when the IT systems and services went live but it does provide a starting point to understand how these systems and services were designed and built. Find out how long ago the project was and what changes have been made to the IT systems and services since then in order to understand how useful or not project documentation may be. It is possible to identify who worked on the projects and if they are still available to interview to find out more about the initial and current state of the IT systems and services. However, if contractors were used they may no longer be available to contact.

If sufficient information has been gathered, once it has been analyzed and reviewed the modeling of the IT systems and services can begin. The model will be used to understand how the IT systems and services will be related within the IT service catalog. An example of a service model from ITIL is provided in figure 5.3. Refer back to figure 5.2 Service catalog schematic for a more detailed service model.

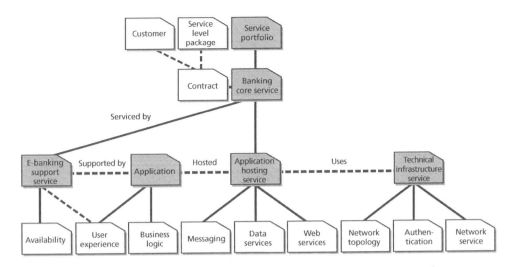

Figure 5.3 ITIL example of a logical configuration model (Source: OGC)

While this is an example of a high level service mapping the IT service catalog needs to go a level below this and show the relationships between the IT systems and how they relate to each other to make up IT services. A big difficulty that can arise is where the IT infrastructure is quite diverse and many different platforms and technologies exist. It is by understanding the services and modeling them in such a way in a diagram that the relationships between the different service catalog types can be identified and understood. Once the basic structure has been indentified it can be set up and mapped within the service catalog. The following list includes a number of key considerations in regards to modeling IT systems and services:

1. Choose a small number of key critical services to model initially. This focuses attention on modeling the important services which is more likely to gain stakeholder, user and customer confidence and support.

2. Ensure that all IT platforms are considered within the initial modeling exercise, even if the initial services that are being mapped do not use some of the platforms. This is to ensure that the service model can support all platforms when non critical services are mapped. Failing to consider all platforms at the initial modeling stage can require extensive remodeling at a later date requiring both time and resources to complete.

3. It is advisable to *proof of concept* the initial model within the IT service catalog application itself to ensure that it is at least feasible to map the model within the application. Following this a prototype of the model can be created, again within the IT service catalog. This will allow the stakeholders, users and customers to see what the end result will look like and to ascertain at an early stage if their requirements can be achieved. If there are problems with either the proof of concept or the prototype the correct action to take is to analyze the problems and identify if the IT service catalog application is actually capable of supporting the requirements. The wrong course of action to take is to change the stakeholder, user and customer requirements to match that what the IT service catalog application can do, as their needs and wants will not be delivered resulting in the IT service catalog being unsuccessful, and unfit for use.

4. To be effective the model of the IT systems and services should support the following capabilities:
   - provide a logical representation/schematic of the systems, services and infrastructure within the IT service catalog
   - provide an impact assessment of systems and services through their relationships
   - facilitate a reporting function to include availability, impact assessment and general reporting

[handwritten: need the mapping to calculate various performance metrics — e.g., meet SLA? Capacity forecasting/planning]

5.3.3 Map

The next step is to map the model into whatever system will retain the IT system and IT service records, i.e. spreadsheet, service catalog application, CMDB. CI records should be related to the IT system records and IT system records should be related to IT service records.

Mapping an IT service catalog within a CMDB

A good CMDB should have the capability to link together CIs, via their CI records. The capability can be utilized to build a basic catalog of IT systems and IT services. Therefore one logical place to build an IT service catalog is within the CMDB. CI records will exist for all IT CIs if the CMDB is mature enough. If the regular upkeep of records is happening the CIs should be up to date. While it may not suit every need, it does fit the purpose of mapping IT systems and services at a minimum. If this is possible from the organization's CMDB, it has the net effect of increasing the organization's ROI from the CMDB. This approach only covers the mapping of service catalog records and does not address any actionable service catalog requirements. If modeled correctly it could also extend to represent business services and customer services, i.e. CI records that are categorized to represent business services and customer services. IT services can then be linked to business services which can be linked to customer services.

A few basic requirements are necessary:

[handwritten margin note: if CMDB is next gen CI provide an actionable capability?]

- CI records exist and are reasonably up to date.
- The CMDB has the ability to make relationships between CIs.
- Relationships can accommodate forward and reverse relationships.

So what are these CI relationships? Quite simply they represent how one CI is connected or related to another. Any decent CMDB will provide the ability to relate CIs to one another. This introduces the concept of *forward and reverse relationships*:

[handwritten: same level mapping?]

- **forward relationship** (up-level):
  - describes how one CI is connected to next CI
  - forward facing from the CI level towards the service level
- **reverse relationship** (down level):
  - describes how one CI is connected to next CI
  - backwards (reverse) facing from the service level towards the CI level

A consideration of note is to check how the CMDB will actually display the relationships so that they can be viewed. Table 5.2 looks a two common ways of displaying relationships within the CMDB.

Type	Advantages	Disadvantages
Hierarchical display (List)	• quick to drill into CIs • less complicated to set up • generally integrated in CMDB	• non visual display of services • may suffer from infinite loops • cannot print service maps • resource intensive to maintain service mappings
Graphical display (Images)	• visual display of services • quick to drill into CIs • possible printing of service maps • may be linked to self discovery tools • automation can be used to maintain service mappings	• may require additional resources to validate and verify data • may require a separate application or integration to achieve a graphical display

Table 5.2 CI relationship views in CMDB systems

does a graph database relate to a graphical display?

The upkeep of these CI relationships is an additional task and responsibility. It will require dedicated resources to ensure that the data is kept valid and up to date. Good change management, CMDB management and service level management practices can help to maintain these service mappings but cannot guarantee it alone. Like the CMDB, IT service mappings are only as up to date as the last time that the data was verified and confirmed as being accurate. One element of responsibility that should be clarified is the role of the service catalog manager in this situation. The service catalog manager still retains overall responsibility for any service catalog that is created within a CMDB and will need to work closely with configuration management to ensure that it is kept up to date and relevant.

5.3.4 Review

It is important to review the initial model and service mapping against the original requirements to ensure that they accurately represent the IT systems and IT services. Before publishing the services and service mappings they need to be reviewed to insure that they are accurate and correct. If they do not, now is the time to redefine requirements, re-evaluate the design, and redo the service mappings. Remember that strong foundations lead to lasting success so plan to get it right from the start and use adequate reviews to ensure quality and accuracy is maintained.

5.3.5 Publish

Publish the IT service catalog within the organization, but note that the audience is generally limited to that of the IT world. In general the organizations staff outside of the IT departments will not need to use this catalog as they will generally not understand it and not want to or need to understand it. Publishing the IT catalog can be as simple as making it available so that it can be used by the relevant people that need to use it. Table 5.3 provides a high level view of the typical audience that can avail from using the IT catalog and the typical role that they may have in IT.

	Administration	Support	Design	Management
IT personnel	x	x		
Support teams	x	x		
Vendor support teams	x	x	x	

	Administration	Support	Design	Management
IT Architects		x	x	
IT Management			x	x

Table 5.3 High view of the typical audience of the IT service catalog.

5.4   Business service catalog design

The business service catalog represents the services that will be used throughout the organization in support of achieving desired and expected business outcomes. The business service catalog should be written and presented in a format understandable by the organization. The business service catalog is the business or organization element of the service catalog that will facilitate the organization in:

- understanding the business services that exist
- understanding the relationships and dependencies between the business services and IT services
- understanding the impact that IT service failures will have on business services
- referencing IT systems to aid in fault resolution and incident management
- mapping out the services that are used by the business in one central repository
- understanding the requirements of service supply and demand within the organization

5.4.1   Requirements

Identify what information is required that needs to be recorded for business service records. At a minimum the following information should be recorded:

- attributes
- status
- service records
- relationships

Description	Detail
Attributes	• Contain the information recorded about the business service. • Workflows (automation) can be triggered from changes in attribute values. • Define attributes that will provide relevant information. • Too many attributes may be difficult to maintain accurately. • Too little may not provide any value. • Each attribute should have an owner who can provide accurate and up to date information for the attribute. • Important attributes should be mandatory. Generally the mandatory requirement is based on the status or other attributes as they change.
Status	• Is an attribute. • Denotes where in the service portfolio lifecycle the service record is.
Service records	• This is the form that contains the information about the business services and contains a relationship to the service level agreement and underpinning contract for that service. • Can be the same form that is used for IT services - but needs to be classified or categorized as a business service record.

Description	Detail
Relationships	• Links business service records to IT service records. • Should have forward and reverse relationships.
Specific information to record	• How the business service is provided? • Whom the business service is provided to? • Who supports the business service? • When is the business service available? • What does the business service actually do?

Ever a where? (handwritten)

Table 5.4 Information that should be recorded in the business service catalog

5.4.2 Model

All business services must be related to the IT services that enable them. It may be possible to relate business services to IT services and the associated IT systems in the same repository. Again, if a multi repository is used it is still vital to make these relationships between the systems that are used to record the service records even though there may be challenges in achieving this easily. The service records that represent the business service should be linked to their associated SLAs. Therefore the business SLAs for the business services should be known and available. If an SLA does not exist for that business service or it has not been covered under an existing SLA, this should be rectified.

is this still true? (handwritten)

Areas that need careful consideration:

• Auto-discovery tools generally cannot be used to identify business services.
• It is a manual task which increases the administration, upkeep and possibility of inaccurate relationships.
• The scope of business services may be vast, especially for larger organizations.
• Identifying key critical business services to be included initially will help focus on the important services first.

If starting out mapping business services for the first time focus on the key critical business services. These may be ones that contribute directly to revenue generating activities or that support legal requirements.

** But not our situation (handwritten)*

5.4.3 Map

Once the business services have been identified, they need to be mapped to the supporting IT service records. The easiest way to do this is to relate the business service records to the IT service records. This should be easy if all the different types of service records are co-located within the one system, for example a fully integrated service catalog or service management system that supports relationships between these records. If the different service record types are stored in different systems then this is going to be more difficult and may require extra administration and system configuration.

5.4.4 Review

Review the initial model and mapping against the original requirements to ensure that they accurately represent the business services. If not, now is the time to re-define, re-evaluate, and re-do. Again, remember that strong foundations lead to lasting success. In chapter two the concept of what constitutes business services was explored. Again neither of these service record types has to be separated in different systems, entities or spreadsheets. They can reside in the one repository differentiated by the service type *business service* or *IT service* but they must be presented to their relevant audience in a format that is understood by the audience.

5.4.5 Publish

Publish the business catalog in the organization. Publishing can be as simple as making it available so that it can be used by the relevant people that need to use it. The users of business services may not need to know of every business service in the organization. However, they should know about the ones that are relevant to them and be able to access the information as required. Management may need to know about the business services and in particular have a need to access SLA information. Information about business services can be made available to users in a static format. One way of doing this is to publish the list of business services within the organizations intranet site or content management system to show the users what services are being provided.

But this would not be actionable [handwritten margin note]

A question that is commonly asked time after time is how to identify the business services and how do all they fit together with IT services?

The answer most commonly found is to take a *top down* approach. The best source of information regarding what business services are in use is the actual users of those services or the business units that rely on the business services. Management may have an idea or an understanding of what business services their staff need and use and should be able to delegate the tasks involved in gathering this information. In large organizations the number of different business services can span in the hundreds or even thousands. Identifying all the different business services within an organization may be a project in itself. At the very least it may require a dedicated person to manage the activities involved in identifying and mapping the business services.

5.5   Customer service catalog design

The customer service catalog represents the services that will be used by the customers of the organization. Like the business service catalog, the customer service catalog should be written and presented in a format understandable by the organization (no tech-speak) and focused on relevance as perceived by the organization and the customers. The customer service catalog is the customer element of the service catalog that will facilitate the organization in:

- understanding the customer services that exist
- understanding the relationships and dependencies between the customer services and the supporting business services and in some cases the directly supporting IT services
- understanding the impact that IT and business service failures will have on customer services
- mapping out the services that are used by customers in one central repository
- understanding customer requirements in regards to service supply and demand
- understanding where customer services are made available (geography, through partners)?

5.5.1 Requirements

Identify what information is required that needs to be recorded for customer service records. At a minimum the following information should be recorded:

- attributes
- status
- service records
- relationships

Description	Detail
Attributes	• Contains the information recorded about the customer service. • Workflows (automation) can be triggered from changes in attribute values. • Define attributes that will provide relevant information. • Too many attributes may be difficult to maintain accurately. • Too little attributes may not provide any value. • Each attribute should have an owner who can provide accurate and up to date information for the attribute. • Important attributes should be mandatory. Generally the mandatory requirement is based on the status or other attributes as they change.
Status	• Is an attribute. • Denotes where in the service portfolio lifecycle the service record is.
Service records	• This is the form that contains the information about the customer services and contains a relationship to the SLA for that service. • Can be the same form that is used for IT services - but needs to be classified or categorized as a business service record.
Relationships	• Links customer service records to business and IT service records. • Should have forward and reverse relationships.
Specific information to record	• How the customer service is provided? • Whom the customer service is provided to? • Who supports the customer service? • When is the customer service available? • What does the customer service actually do?

Table 5.5 Information that should be recorded in the customer service catalog

5.5.2 Model

Customer services are related to the business services that are used to support them and in some cases may be directly related to IT services that enable specific technical functions. It may be possible to relate customer service records to the business and IT service records the same repository. Again, if a multi repository is used it is still vital to make these relationships between the systems that are used to record the service records even though there may be challenges in achieving this easily.

The service records that represent the customer service should be linked to any relevant contractual agreements that may exist between the organization and its customers for that service. There may be terms and conditions that apply to the customers for using a customer service which should also be linked to/from the customer service record. Also, there may be a service level agreement in place between internal service providers and/or internal and external (third party) service providers. Therefore these should be documented and related to the customer service record. If any of these documents do not exist for a customer service this should be rectified.

is this still true?

Areas that need careful consideration:

- Auto-discovery tools generally cannot be used to identify customer services.
- It is a manual task which increases the administration, upkeep and possibility of inaccurate relationships.
- The scope of customer services may be vast, especially for larger organizations.
- Identifying key critical customer services to be included initially will help focus on the important services first.

> If starting out mapping customer services for the first time focus on the key critical customer services. As with business services these may be ones that contribute directly to revenue generating activities or that support legal requirements.

5.5.3 Map

Once the customer services have been identified, they need to be mapped to the supporting business and IT service records. The easiest way to do this is to relate the customer service records to the business and IT service records. This should be easy if all the different types of service records are co-located within the one system, for example a fully integrated service catalog or service management system that supports relationships between these records. If the different service record types are stored in different systems then this is going to be more difficult and may require extra administration and system configuration.

5.5.4 Review

Review the initial model and mapping against the original requirements to ensure that they accurately represent the customer services. If not, now is the time to re-define, re-evaluate, and re-do. Again, remember that strong foundations lead to lasting success. In chapter two the concept of what constitutes customer services was explored. Again none of these service record types have to be separated in different systems, entities or spreadsheets. They can reside in the one repository differentiated by the service type *customer, business* or *IT service records* but they must be presented to their relevant audience in a format that is understood by the audience.

5.5.5 Publish

Are customer services published in the same manner as business services? The short answer is yes. The customer service records are certainly published within the organization so that there is a record of the customer services that the organization provides and that these services can be directly related to the various businesses and IT services that enable them. The actual services that are made available to customers will be provided from customer actionable service catalogs.

so they are definitely actionable

5.6   Actionable service catalog design

The service catalog types discussed in the previous sections are all concerned with recording information about services and their relationships. The actionable service catalogs provide interfaces to users and customers from which they can use specific services that are provided to them.

5.6.1 Business and customer actionable catalog

The main difference between the business and customer actionable catalog is that the business actionable catalog provides interfaces that can be used by the organizations users to use specific services that are provided internally within the organization while the customer actionable catalog provides interfaces that can be used by the organizations customers to use specific services that are provided externally from the organization. In some cases there can be little difference between the interfaces that these two actionable catalogs are built on. In other cases it is possible to find that customer actionable catalogs can be provided using specific, feature rich applications and functionality while the business actionable catalog may not. In such cases the strategy is generally to spend the necessary funds that will provide a feature rich, user friendly customer actionable catalog that allows business revenues to grow by encouraging more customers to avail of the organizations services. The return on investment (ROI) may be easier to quantify for this strategy based on increases in revenue from customers using the customer actionable catalog interfaces to do business with the organization. Internal business actionable catalogs may not be as easy to quantify an ROI and therefore may not be as feature rich or even properly funded. There are basic elements of any actionable service catalog that require careful consideration which include:

• entitlement
• security
• language
• popularity

5.6.2 Entitlement

It is vital that only the people that should be able to access the actionable service catalog are entitled. Entitlement is the process whereby users and customers are authorized to have the appropriate level of access and rights in order to carry out a business process or customer service. In regards to the business actionable catalog certain employees may have limited access to the common and most frequently actionable business services. Departments may have specific actionable services that only they can access and use. Entitlement is generally controlled by roles which are assigned to user accounts. In relation to the customer actionable catalog this may mean that certain countries cannot access the catalog. Examples could include, trade embargos or a limited distribution and supply chain to certain countries or requiring customers to register before being able to use the actionable services.

5.6.3 Security

This is an important consideration when customers are ordering goods and services from the customer actionable catalog. A secure payment method is required and can be facilitated by utilizing smart technology, for example a secure transfer protocol or a trusted source. Also information that is stored about customers must be handled and maintained in a secure manner and should adhere to the relevant data protection acts that exist for the countries where the organization is providing the services. Data integrity is vital in order to ensure customer confidence and loyalty. Only one security incident is enough to cause customers to lose confidence in an organization and seek to do business with competitors in particular if a security breach involves personal information such as name, address, bank details and social security details.

5.6.4 Language

Whether it is the internal business actionable catalog or the customer actionable catalog ensure the correct localization of language - where providing actionable services in different countries - to mitigate against problems such as language and understanding.

5.6.5 Popularity (ease of use)

In order to be successful, the actionable service catalog should be designed in such a way that it encourages both users and customers to come back and use it time after time. Users repeatedly using the business actionable catalog will justify the cost to the organization in providing the services and increase the ROI. User productivity can be increased as requests can be handled and processed quicker, faster and smarter, for example by utilizing intelligent workflows for processing requests. An example of this is a user logging a service request or resetting passwords via a web portal.

Customers returning to an organization's website and ordering or re-ordering goods and services contribute to the organization's finances and also increase the ROI from the actionable customer service catalog. A key element to any web based strategy for a customer actionable catalog is to make it as easy as possible for the customer to do business with the organization from the most user-friendly environment that is possible. An example of this is Amazon.com. The Amazon. com interface is just so easy to use and navigate and it even recommends choices to the customer based on previous experience. Customers can manage their own accounts and track their orders to exactly where they are at that point in time. Many other sites have now duplicated this functionality and make it so easy for the customer to do business with an organization.

5.7   Examples

5.7.1 Service catalog schematic - example

Figure 5.4 applies an example to the service catalog schematic. The premise of this example is based on an organization that provides, amongst others, online banking services to their customers.

As previously discussed it may be possible to record the various service catalog records within the CMDB/CMS, provided that it has the capability to record the information about the services, classify the different service records and to make relationships between the various service catalog records. The blue arrows represent the relationships between the service records. These relationships should mirror how the services are built and will document the forward and reverse relationships discussed in section 5.3.3 Map.

Note: this example places *Email* as an IT service which is provided to users within the business service *Communication services* as part of a bundle that includes *Instant Messaging*. Each department is not charged individually for email or instant messaging but instead charged for the business service *Communication services* which bundles together the IT services. It is easier for the departments to understand the service that is provided and what they are being charged for. If email was the only communication service being provided to the organization then it is likely that there would be two service records for email. An IT service record would contain the relationships to IT systems and a business service record would represent the email service from the user perspective.

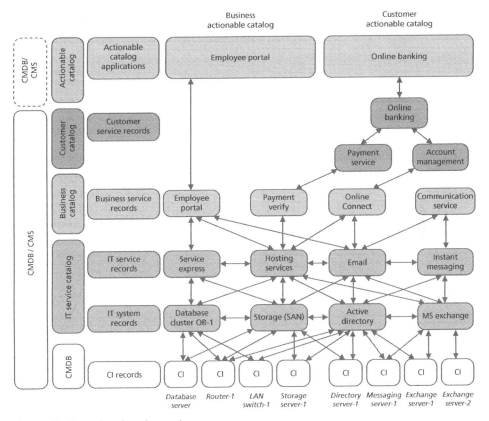

Figure 5.4 Service catalog schematic example

Employee portal

In this example the "Employee portal" provides the interface for using the business actionable catalog. This is the actual service that is made available to the users. As this service is used internally within the organization, there are no customer service records related to, or needed for, this service. In the business service catalog, there is a business service record created called "Employee portal". The purpose of this business service record is to record all the relevant information about the "Employee portal" service. In this case, there is no service used by the organizations staff outside of IT to administer the portal so no other business service records exist which reference administration services. The employee portal requires a number of IT services, namely service express, hosting services and email. The IT service records contain all the relevant information in individual service records about each of the IT services that are required to provide the business service. A brief explanation of the IT services is provided in table 5.6.

IT service	Description
Service express	This is the IT service that provides all the various applications, integrations and platforms etc. that are needed in order to provide the Employee Portal. It is at an IT level and will generally contain IT specific information.
Hosting services	The hosting service is a fundamental and required capability that IT provides which is needed to provide the Employee Portal.
Email	The employee portal sends email alerts to the relevant approvers when items are ordered through the service catalog and relies on the Email service in order to do this. The portal also includes a support form that, once completed and submitted, will send an email to the relevant support group with the details.

Table 5.6 IT Services from service catalog schematic example

Each IT service is built from a collection of IT systems. IT system records record the information about each individual IT system and also maintains the relations between the CIs that are needed to provide the IT system. This is typically what traditional CMDBs would record. There are many to many relationships at this level as IT infrastructure can be highly integrated and many CI components shared. At the CI level router-1 is shared by multiple IT systems in order for the IT systems to be able to route data. Active directory, an IT system, requires multiple CIs to work and is required by multiple IT services for them to work also.

Online banking

In this example *online banking* provides the interface for using the customer actionable catalog. This is the actual service that is made available to the customers of the organization which allows customers to access their banking details and use the various services that are provided to them. As this service is used externally to the organization, there are customer service records related to the service. The *online banking* customer service record contains all the information, non technical, about the service that is provided to the customer. It also contains 2 additional services called *payment services* and *account management*. These are critical services that the customers can use when online. They have separate customer service records as they each require different business services in order to function. Each customer service record will contain specific information regarding these customer services. The business service *payment verify* is used by internal staff to administer the customer services *payment services*. *Payment verify* requires *hosting services* (IT service) in order to work and *hosting services* requires the four IT systems for it to work, and so on. This level of information, detail and service mapping provides a complete end to end understanding of the organizations services at all levels. This is the ideal decomposition of services using the different service catalog types in order to break down each service into an understandable and relevant format. The product, professional services and supplier service catalogs have not been referenced in this example but easily fit into the schematic by their relationship to each service catalog type.

To recap briefly a number of basic but important rules to take note of are:
- Ensure stakeholder, user and customer involvement from the start.
- Ensure stakeholders, users and customers validate that their requirements throughout the design, build and test stages.
- Identify what information is relevant and will provide value.
- Assign overall owners to the various service catalog types.

(handwritten margin note: what would this look like for cloud environments / virtual machines)

- Don't expect to have all the information completed at the first attempt.
- Ensure accurate and up to date information is held in the service records.
- Be capable of analyzing and reporting the information stored about services.
- Build in the ability to report on what information is complete within the service catalog and the service records and what is still outstanding. *– what are we looking for?*
- Audit the service catalog repositories on a regular basis.
- Ensure that services are recorded as early as possible.
- Identify areas for improvement right from the start and continually look for ways to improve.
- Communicate, communicate, communicate; let people know where they can access the different service catalogs.
- Location, location, location; place the different service catalogs somewhere relevant and accessible by the intended audience.
- Use what is relevant for your organization; there is no universal service catalog template or design.
- Keep the momentum going; don't let the service catalog be today's fad, but forgotten about tomorrow.

5.7.2 Actionable service catalog example

Section 2.5 provides a table that details the basic information that should be recorded for the various service records. The actionable service catalog is an interface that provides services to users and customers. Figure 5.5 is an example of a business actionable service catalog. The diagram is kept basic to highlight the main parts. The catalog could be presented via a thick client or through a web page. The functionality discussed in this section may be provided by an application or could be built and integrated into existing systems or platforms.

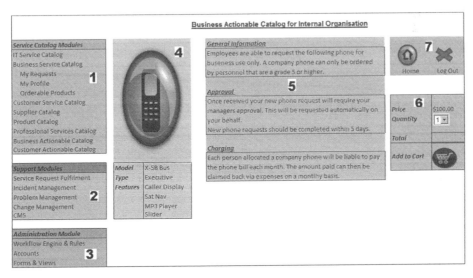

Figure 5.5 Business actionable catalog

1. **Service catalog modules** - This section lists the available service catalogs. Depending on the authorization a user has when logged into the system, they may not get to see all the service catalog types available. In this example the business service catalog has additional options for the end-user to choose from.

2. **Support modules** - This section is relevant to the IT support function in the organization. It should be obvious that in this example a number of service management support processes are listed. The support personnel would have access to these, but neither the organizations end-users nor their customers would have access. They should not even see these sections as they are not directly relevant to them. The service requests would be shown in a separate section with a particular view for the end-user or customer. Refer to chapter 2.5 Service records, in particular the service catalog record example which looks at process relationships.

3. **Administration modules** - This is the section of the system where all configurations and administrative tasks take place. Different systems will have different configurability options and possibilities. Therefore it is crucial that the organization, including the service catalog stakeholders, know what is required and needed from each of the service catalog types before deciding on the final technology solution. Don't let the chosen applications or systems become a barrier to achieving required outcomes.

Workflow is a crucial element in regards to the actionable service catalogs. It is the engine that drives the automation of each request from creating the service request to driving approvals and notifications. Workflow will help reduce administrative tasks only if it has been developed with maximizing efficiencies and effectiveness in mind. Get the workflow wrong and bottlenecks could be introduced increasing the time required to fulfill requests. The technology solution may be a combination of multiple applications, systems and platforms.

4. **Product information** - Details about the available products can be provided to the users and customers. This information can be pulled directly from the product catalog. It is also possible to integrate or imbed the product catalog in the actionable service catalog.

5. **User information** - This section in the example provides the user with additional information that is useful to know. An important point to make with respect to the approvals of requests in that workflow should be used to reduce the administration of the approvals process. Approvals can be different for each request type and therefore it makes sense to automate this where feasible.

6. **Product selection (cart)** - This is a simple function that allows the user or customer to add the item selection(s) to their cart, view the details at a later stage and to verify chosen products before submitting the request. The function is the same whether it is used by users or customers and is fairly standard in any good business or customer actionable service catalog.

7. **Menu options** - These help the user and customer navigate through the system. A number of key navigation buttons should be provided.

What is not visible from the interface is the ability to report on the activities of the users and customers. In this example is should be relatively easy to report on:

- How many phone units were deployed to the organizations staff.
- Who they were deployed to.
- Who authorized them for use.
- What department or cost centre should be charged for the units.
- How long it took for users to receive the phone unit.
- How many follow up calls the user had to log to the service desk in order to complete the request and/or set up the phone to a working state.
- The depreciation value of the phone units based on their purchase date.

5.7.3 Actionable catalog process example - order process

In the previous example the product catalog has been used to identify what phones are available and a particular phone has been selected by the user to order. To be able to process the phone order made by the user, workflow will be required within the actionable service catalog in order to automate the fulfillment of this request from the actionable service catalog. Some areas for consideration are as follows:

Considerations	Details (Applicable to order phone workflow)
Will anyone be allowed to order a phone?	Yes. If not, entitlement needs to be understood. Who can order the item and how will this be validated and controlled?
Will there be an approval mechanism?	Yes.
Who can approve requests?	Line managers as listed in directory services.
How will people approve the request?	An automatic approval work order will be generated and assigned to the appropriate line manager. The work order will be automatically linked to the service request using the API.
What happens if the request is not approved?	The line manager will continue to receive approval notifications every two days until the approval work order is approved or rejected.
How will the user be kept informed?	At defined intervals the service request status will be updated to reflect where the request is within the order process. The status will be visible to the requestor from their personal page within the service catalog. Note: more advanced systems can offer more advanced functionality in this area, for example Amazon can track where your order is at any given time.
How does the actual request get processed from start to finish?	As per the process flow.
Identify bottlenecks.	Line managers not approving work orders. Delays in purchasing requisitions being completed in a timely manner.

Table 5.7 Order phone workflow considerations

The key point is to understand and map out the actual process from start to finish in order to be able to understand what workflows are required to automate the process as much as possible.

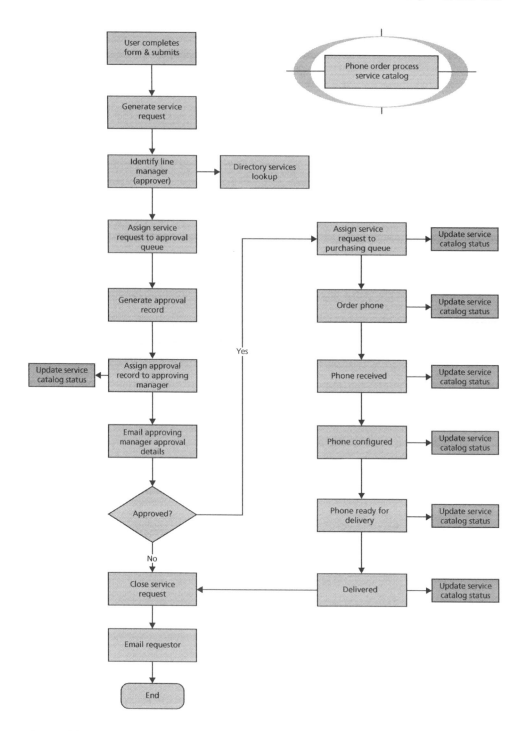

Figure 5.6 "Phone order" process

6 Management and organization

The service catalog provides a central source of information regarding all services that are currently being provided to the organization and its customers. The information contained within the service catalog should be managed, maintained and updated on a regular basis in order to provide value back to the organization. Ongoing management of the service catalog is critical. After all, what value can be provided from a service catalog, or any other management system, that is not up to date and which does not reflect the current environment accurately?

Key information that the service catalog should contain on a service by service basis includes service level requirements, service level targets and service level agreements. This means that there are direct links, interfaces and dependencies between the service catalog and the service level management process. Therefore, this chapter includes information on the service level management process and elements of the process that are required in order to ensure that services have appropriate levels of utility and warranty that ensures they are fit for purpose and fit for use. Information is also included on a number of additional roles that are required to ensure that both the service catalog and the services themselves are managed correctly. Ongoing management of the services is also required. Overtime, requirements will change, demand levels may rise or fall and new technologies will enable new services and streamline existing or older services.

6.1 Service catalog management process

It takes an abundance of coordination and effort in order to correctly design, populate and update the various service catalogs and all their different elements and service types. It takes very little time for any of the information or relationships in any of the service catalogs to become old, out of date or obsolete. Therefore it is imperative to ensure that there are measures in place that are robust enough to ensure that all this information and the service record relationships are kept valid, up to date and remain relevant to the needs of the organization.

To some it is seen that *strong governance* of the service catalog is required. In reality what is required is *strong management* of the service catalog. The service portfolio and service catalog are only as up to date as the last update that was made to them. Strict management practices are required. So, in effect another *process* or *sub process* is required in order to manage keeping the service catalog up to date, relevant, accurate, useful and representative of the true state of all services in the organization. ITIL introduced a new process called *service catalog management* within the Service Design book. The following is outlined within the Service Design book in regards to service catalog management:

Service catalog management	Description
Purpose	Single source of consistent information on services.
Goal	Ensure that the service catalog is produced and maintained containing accurate information on all services throughout the service lifecycle.
Objective	Manage the information contained within the service catalog throughout the service lifecycle.

Table 6.1 Service catalog management: purpose, goal and objectives

The following diagram represents the key elements of any process that can and will support any of the service catalog types. This diagram is explained in detail in Appendix A.

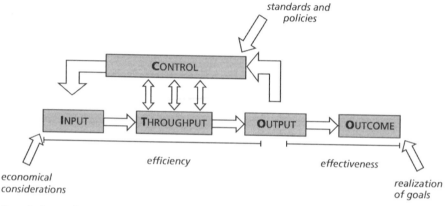

Figure 6.1 Process diagram, based on the ITOCO-model

This section details elements that would be expected to be found in a process, which can be applied to the development of the service catalog management process. It is still up to the organization to develop a process that is fit for their individual purpose and fit for their individual use which is aligned to the needs and outcomes of the organization. This section acts as a starting point for such organizations. There are a number of elements that a process document should cover. At a minimum, the process should include the following sections:

- scope and objectives
- process flow
- process narrative
- roles and responsibilities
- appendices

6.1.1 Scope
In effect the service catalog is the scope. It should be defined whether the process covers the management of the entire service portfolio, i.e. the service pipeline, service catalog and the retired services elements or just the service catalog. There may be separate processes (or sub-processes) to manage each of the different service catalogs including the technical, business, customer and actionable service catalogs.

6.1.2 Objective
The service catalog is to be kept relevant and up to date on a regular and continual basis. The process should detail how to manage the information contained within the service catalog throughout the service lifecycle.

6.1.3 Process flow
Detail the inputs, activities and outputs of the process. This could be in the form of a process follow or swim lane diagram (some organizations have a preference for one of these over the other). The overall *outcome* of this process is to ensure that the processes objectives are met.

6.1.4 Process narrative
The process narrative should list each process step and include:
- the process step name and number
- the roles that can perform the process step
- description of the step
- additional details required to understand the step in detail

6.1.5 Roles and responsibilities
Roles and responsibilities should be clearly defined and are made available to those involved in the process. Otherwise, how is one to know where responsibility lies in the execution of the various process steps. See section 6.7 "Ownership and roles" for additional information.

6.1.6 Appendices
This section should include relevant supporting information. Appendices can be used to document very specific details about the overall process or supporting information to the process narrative.

In the execution of the process, the support personnel involved will not want to have to read through a large process document to understand the process. However, for support personnel they can focus their attention on just the process flow and the process narrative. This will greatly increase their awareness of the process. The rest of the process document is there to support the management of the process and provide the in-scope and out-of-scope boundaries for the process owner, process manager and anyone in the organization that has a need to know.

6.2   Service catalog management process flow

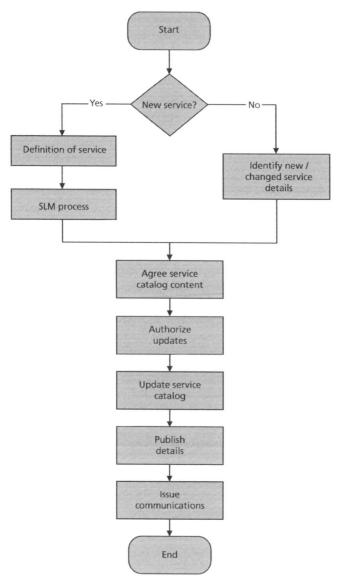

Figure 6.2 Example of a service catalog management process

Due to the diverse nature of organizations and the way that they are likely to implement the various service catalog types it is highly likely that processes to manage the overall service catalog are likely to differ from organization to organization. Because of this, it will be difficult to provide a "one size fits all" processes for the service catalog.

Figure 6.2 is an example of a very simple process flow that can be used to manage updates to the service catalog records. Large organizations may require a more advanced service catalog management process due to their size and complex structure while smaller organization may require such a lean approach. Overly complex process flows can be cumbersome and cause administrative overhead while too simplistic processes can be ineffective. What organizations share in common is that each organization will have to tailor an appropriate service catalog management processes that fits their needs, their organization and structure, and above all will provide processes and procedures that are suitable to manage their specific service catalog be it spreadsheets, word documents, databases or specific service catalog applications. Additional information regarding processes is provided in Appendix A.

This example details the basic process activities in regards to adding new and changing content and information to the service catalog. Section 6.5.5 provides an example of a service focused service level management process which should be used if the answer to the "New service?" step is "yes". Section 6.6 "Interfaces with ITIL or ITSM disciplines" provides the ITIL view of processes and functions that interface with the service catalog.

6.3   Service catalog audit process

Not only does the service catalog need to be updated when new services are introduced and existing services change, it is important for the information contained within the service catalog to be audited. Auditing and verification of the service catalog provides a means to evaluate if the service catalog management process is being followed, if it is effective and if the information about all the services is accurate, up to date and relevant. Inaccurate information is worthless and can cause many issues. For example, not correctly updating the price that will be charged for a service may lead the user or customer being charged the incorrect price leading to disputes and potentially a loss of user and customer confidence. Not having the correct information within the technical service catalog may lead to issues in designing and developing services or affect the quality of Business Impact Assessments (BIA). Inaccurate information regarding business services, service owners, pricing etc. may affect the relationship between the business and IT.

Therefore another important process to put in place is a process that will audit the service catalog and the information contained within it. If the organization already has an auditing process it should be possible to apply it to, and use it for, the auditing of the service catalog. If not figure 6.3 provides an example of audit process that is not overly complex but can be used to sufficiently audit the service catalog. The process is split into three distinct phases:
- pre audit
- conduct audit
- audit corrective action

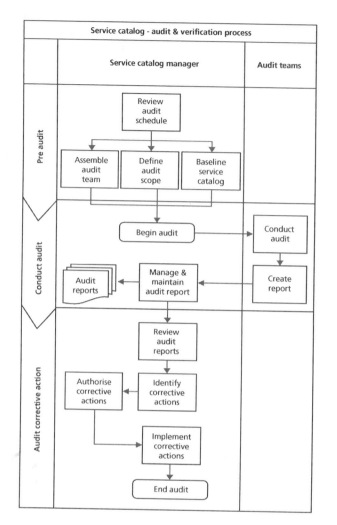

Figure 6.3 Service catalog audit process

Pre audit

The service catalog manager should maintain a service catalog audit review schedule that defines when the service catalog audits will take place. When an audit is due the service catalog manager assembles the audit team, defines the scope of the audit and creates a baseline of the service catalog.

Conduct audit

The audit team carries out the audit, analyses the data and documents the findings in the audit report. The report is provided to the service catalog manager for review. The service catalog manager is accountable for managing the overall service catalog report.

Audit corrective action

The service catalog manager reviews the audit report and identifies corrective actions that are necessary to address the findings. The service catalog manager will also work with the relevant management within the organization in order to agree how to address the findings and once a plan has been established, will authorize the corrective actions and ensure that agreed measures are implemented as planned.

Items that should be audited are listed in Table 6.2. While a single individual audit does not have to include the entire audit areas listed below, nonetheless they should be targeted to be audited over a period of time.

Audit Area	Details
Service attribute data	The information about each service that is recorded within the service records should be reviewed to make sure that it is correct, relevant and up to date. Also the review should consider if any attributes are missing, whereby providing information on missing attributes in the future would provide value to the users of the service catalog. Inaccurate data provides no value while important data needs to be captured and recoded.
Service relationships	The relationships between the different service record types should be audited to make sure that they are correct and that they represent the correct configuration / mapping of each service. Incorrect service mappings will affect the accuracy of business impact assessments and may lead to inaccurate charging of services amongst other issues.
Documentation	Process, procedures, work instructions, reports, service level agreements, operational level agreement, and underpinning contracts are documents that help achieve desired service catalog outcomes in a formalized manner and should be audited to ensure that they are efficient and effective and are updated in line with organizational change.
People	Are the correct people involved in the service catalog management process? Do the other processes and relevant personnel interface with the service catalog and the service catalog management process including the service catalog process owner, service catalog manager, service owners, service level managers. People play a key role in the success of any process and their participation and interaction in each process is vital to ensure the achievement of KPI's and CSF's and the efficient and effective execution and management of the process.
Products / technology	The technology that is used to provide the service catalog and actionable service catalog workflows, interface and usability should also be audited to ensure that it remains fit for purpose and fit for use and that the technology is aligned to changes in both processes and desired business outcomes.

Table 6.2 Audit items

6.4   Request fulfillment

ITIL positions the request fulfillment process as the process that deals with completing user and customer service requests. It is this process that is responsible for completing service requests logged via the business or customer actionable catalog. Request fulfillment can be a very simple thing. At the same time it can be a very complex matter indeed. However the main outcome of fulfilling requests is a satisfied user or customer with their request completed on time and as expected. Request fulfillment was, in previous ITIL versions, part of the incident management process. However, request fulfillment is now its own distinct process and therefore it is a perfect fit for dealing with requests logged via the actionable service catalog. The actionable service catalog can be used as a portal for logging service requests. In ITIL request fulfillment is concerned with completing service requests and has been defined as:

> *(Service Operation) "The process responsible for managing the lifecycle of all Service Requests."*

ITIL states that the objectives of the request fulfillment process are as follows:

> *(Service Operation).*
> - *To provide a channel for users to request and receive standard services for which a pre-defined approval and qualification process exists*
> - *To provide information to users and customers about the availability of services and the procedure for obtaining them*
> - *To source and deliver the components of requests standard services (for example licenses and software media)*
> - *To assist with general information, complaints or comments*

Basically, request fulfillment is the process by which end-user's requests (or customer's requests) are handled to completion. It is that simple in context but can be very complex due to the nature of the requests that need to be serviced. Remember that in the eyes of the end-user or the customer, all they want is to have their request completed:
- as quickly as possible
- as seamlessly as possible
- with the minimum of fuss, hassle or their involvement

Request fulfillment can be a manual set of tasks and activities that need to take place in order to complete the request and satisfy the users or customers. However, by utilizing the most appropriate technology correctly, it is possible to automate various elements of the request fulfillment process. This can effectively reduce handling times, errors and waiting periods for end-users and customers.

The following table provides some examples of different internal and external services that an organization may provide to end-users and customers. These services would typically be handled under the request fulfillment process and the access management process in the case of resetting password. These are also examples of services that can be offered via the actionable service catalog.

Internal services (end-user)	External services (customer)
Reset password - for any number of systems.	Reset password - generally for the actual internet site but can be for other systems and provided services also.
Order a new laptop.	Order goods, products or services.
Log an incident or service request.	Return ordered goods.
Request an increase in email file size.	Contact customer service.
Release filtered/quarantined email.	Chat with a customer service representative.

Internal services (end-user)	External services (customer)
Personalize content.	Provide shopping cart facilities.
Direct content personally to the employee based on department, unit, business area, et cetera.	Payment facilities.
On-board of new staff.	Ability to personalize content.
Invoke deactivation.	Account management.
Content and usability can be restricted to roles, location, access rights, security requirements, et cetera.	Content can be personally directed to customers in an effort to increase sales.

Table 6.3 Example of different internal and external services

A common misconception is that once a service request is logged what happens behind the scenes is not necessarily important for the requestor to know about. Wrong! Confidence is critical in winning over people's perception that a quality service is being provided. Even more important is that the person feels they have been listened to, understood and that the organization cares about them. It is quite likely that the end-user/customer will have more confidence that their request is being handled and managed correctly. The more informed the requestor is in regards where their request is, the less likely they are to call a support desk to find out the status of the request. This frees up time spent chasing the status, location and update of requests and allows support staff to focus on other priority tasks and duties.

Be sure to set the users or customers expectations as early as possible in regards to the level of service that they will receive. Failing to set their expectations may lead to them creating their own expectation. This "*self set" expectation* can generally be higher than that which can be offered by the organization. Failing to deliver the outcome as expected by the user or customer can lead to their dissatisfaction even if the request was handled as expected. A number of common scenarios are as follows:
- The request was handled incorrectly.
- The request was handled correctly but the end-user or customer's expectation did not match what was being offered.
- The request fulfillment process is flawed.
- Automation used to reduce manual tasks and activities is set up incorrectly.
- The expectation of the end-user or customer was higher than what was being provided.

It is important that the user or customer expectation is set from the start of their experience or interaction with the request fulfillment process. Failing to do so will generally result in dissatisfaction and failing to meet the end-user's or customer's conditions of satisfaction. If the customer's expectations are not set from the start it is likely that they will create their own expectation. If the answer to the question "Do you have SLAs in your organization?" is "no" that does not mean that users or customers do not have their own expectations of the service. What can happen is that in the absence of SLA's, or published SLA's that outline the level of service provision that is to be delivered, the organization may have to deal with the fact that the customer will assume what the levels of service are based on their expectations.

Have you ever bought a DVD online and used the facility that allows you to track precisely where the order is during transit? If so, did you feel more confident that the item would be delivered? Did you also feel more in control by knowing when the item would be delivered and where exactly it was? If you expected it to be delivered within two days but were told that due to unexpected demand the product would be delayed by a number of days, would you feel less annoyed about the situation as you are aware that there is a reason behind the delay? And were you happy to find all of this information from the same place where you logged the original request?

Have you ever had to call customer service and log a request, complaint or query? If yes, did you feel more confident that the request would be handled if you could see the status and updates online? Did you feel that the organization cared about you just that little bit more? Provided that the user or customer is kept informed and up to date throughout the entire experience there should be less reason for dissatisfaction. Due to human nature, dissatisfaction can never be totally abolished. However, the key to success is to reduce the negative impact to users and customers alike.

The actionable service catalog can be used to allow users and customers to interact with the organization by using services. Different services can and will be offered depending on whether a user or a customer is the recipient of that service. Standard formatting and presentation rules apply. An understanding of the activities and tasks that are required in order to complete a service request from end-to-end, or put another way, from start to finish is needed. The activities that happen in between need to be fully understood. If not, how are these service requests to be completed efficiently and effectively either manually or via automated workflows? Equally the underlying support structures must be in place to ensure that the user request can be completed, preferably on time and within expected budget.

An example of the request fulfillment process for a specific scenario is provided in section 5.7.3 "Actionable catalog process example – order process". Additional details regarding request fulfillment and the request fulfillment process can be obtained from the ITIL Service Operations book from OGC.

6.5   Service level management

Service level management is one of the key disciplines by which an organization manages their services. Service level management acts as the interface between IT and the business. It is involved in the linking of IT services and business services. Chapter two introduced the concept that the service catalog consists of the following service types:

* customer services
* business services
* IT services
* IT systems

The IT service catalog consists of IT services and IT systems. The business service catalog consists of the services used by the business that are provided by IT systems and services. The linking of these two worlds is a key responsibility of service level management. It should be a key requirement in the organization at senior management level to ensure that this happens. This should not come across as a radical approach at all. Service level management has a key role to play in achieving this unification but is not the only role involved. See section 6.7 "Ownership and roles" for information regarding additional roles.

Service level management should not just be focused on IT services, but needs to deal with customer and business services as well. If not, service level management runs the risk of just being IT focused and not business or customer focused. ITIL positions service level management as a process. However, due to the scope of what is involved in service level management its scope can span that beyond what can be defined in an end-to-end process. The process element of service level management should define the main inputs, activities and outputs of the process. The success of service level management is dependent on the quality of the service catalog and its contents. The service catalog provides necessary information about the services that are managed by the service level management process. At the most basic level service level management is involved in the following activities:

- **Define** levels of service.
- **Agree** levels of service.
- **Record** levels of service.
- **Manage** levels of service.

Service level management ensures that:
- an agreed level of service is provided for each service
- new services are brought online to agreed service level targets
- all parties have a clear understanding of service level targets
- service level agreements are negotiated, agreed and signed off
- service level agreements exist and are aligned to meet the business requirements that support desired business outcomes
- all targets and measures contained within service level agreements are supported by appropriate underpinning contracts and operational level agreements
- service levels are monitored and reported to make certain that they are achieved and that corrective action is identified where service levels are not met
- adequate relationships exist throughout the organization, its suppliers and customers
- bottlenecks are identified and remedial action implemented
- the needs of the organization and its customers are identified and understood

Service level management plays an important role in the continual service improvement of services. As time goes by it is highly probable that customers change, markets change, regulatory requirements change, organizations change, technologies change, and so on. Further, as you might expect, services may also have to change to still be relevant in an ever changing environment. Therefore services need to be reviewed on an ongoing basis against customer and business needs to ascertain if service level requirements have changed. A service that was implemented two years ago may not meet the requirements of the organization or its users or customers today. However, before embarking on a program of service improvement an organization needs to be capable of measuring service performance. This will, in-effect, become the baseline against which service improvement initiatives can show their success (or failure).

Service reviews should be scheduled well in advance. Service level management should prepare a pre-planned schedule of service reviews. This links directly back to the service catalog. The service catalog plays an important part in the review of services. It is the main repository of information relating to all known or documented services. Each service record should contain the date of the next service review for that service. Once done, the service catalog now has a list of all service review dates for each service listed, which provides the service review schedule. Section 2.5 "Service records" contains an example of a service record that includes a field that captures the date that both the service and the service record was last reviewed. This date field can be used within a report to analyze those services and service records that have not been reviewed within certain time periods e.g. within the last six or twelve months.

Note: once a new service develops from something more than just an idea it is imperative that, at these initial stages, a new service is recorded in the service portfolio under the service pipeline element. This ensures that as the service plans develop, the service will be managed throughout the service lifecycle from cradle to grave, i.e. from inception to end. The service record can act as a central reference point for information relating to the service. It is highly improbable that all information relating to the service will be able to be stored in the service pipeline repository. However it is quite probable to store the links to such information easily within the service record thus acting as a central reference point for information relating to the service. At such an early stage the status should refer to the service being at a conceptual stage or at the initial stages of development. This ensures that the organization has an initial entry in the service portfolio so the service can now be tracked throughout its lifecycle and the information about the service from this early stage right up to it going live can be assessable from the service record.

The following are broad generalizations, not in line with best practice, that unfortunately re-appear time after time:
• Service level management is generally associated with service level agreements.
• Service level agreements are often confused with service level targets.
• Service level targets are often referred to as *the SLA or service level agreement.*
• It is common to have no service level agreement defined for a service that is live.
• It is common for organizations to have in-complete or in-effective service level agreements or worse still, none at all.

There are a number of key elements that are required to ensure that services are fit for purpose and fit for use and remain so throughout their lifetime. These are:
• service level requirements
• service level targets
• service level agreements

Figure 6.4 shows the order in which these should follow:

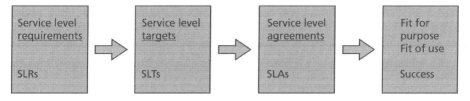

Figure 6.4 Order to ensure services are fit for purpose and fit for use

These key elements are discussed in more detail in the following sections.

6.5.1 Service level requirements

The following provides various definitions of a **service level requirement**:

Frameworks	Service level requirements definitions
Service Design	A customer requirement for an aspect of an IT service. SLRs are based on business objectives and are used to negotiate agreed service level targets.
MOF	Cross reference ITIL V3 and MOF 4.0 Service requirements and service level requirements (SLR) (both terms are used in ITIL). Like in ITIL, both terms are used in MOF, in various activities, processes, and SMFs, like reliability (PLAN), financial management (PLAN), service monitoring and control (OPERATE). Business requirements: used in the service level management process in the business-IT alignment SMF; in the "define service requirements" activity in process 1: planning in the reliability SMF (PLAN); and in MRs like project plan approved (DELIVER), service alignment (PLAN)
ISO/IEC 20000-1:2005	The first step, in concluding SLAs about the IT services provided today or in the future, should be to identify and define the customer needs in the service level requirements. Besides doing so once within the course of the process, this activity should also be carried out regularly, initiated by reports and reviews, at the request of the customer or for the benefit of the IT organization. The activity may cover new or existing services.
USMBOK	Customer side influences Service level requirements: representing the finalized service level requirements communicated to the customer community.

Table 6.4 Framework definitions of service level requirements

Basically, to understand the service level requirements means that the organization's users and customers needs and wants are understood. These requirements should then be turned into reality, though sometimes the initial requirements get re-translated within the context and confines of the service provider's capability to deliver or within the budget available. Neither of these realities is ideal in achieving the organizations outcomes, but they are a reality nonetheless.

It is vital from the start to have a clear understanding of what is the need for the particular service from the user or customer view. The organization may also have requirements that need to be taken into consideration. Getting these wrong, making incorrect assumptions, or failing to understand basic requirements at an early stage can cause severe problems throughout the life of the service. The service level management process is responsible for identifying service level requirements that will eventually feed into the service level agreement for the service. These need to be negotiated and agreed and a formal service level agreement put in place. Change management should be used to move the service into the production environment and to manage that service throughout its lifetime.

It is worth noting that users and customers may not know themselves what exactly they require from the service. There may be a level of simple assumptions made on their part, in that the service will provide basic functions that they expect. So simply asking the question "what are your requirements?" may not be nearly enough. It may require a good understanding of the service coupled with excellent user and customer relationships in order to identify accurate and meaningful service level requirements. See section 4.4.4 for additional information on techniques that can be used when identifying requirements. In addition service level requirements need to be judged in the context of the value of the service. If the cost of meeting an availability level for a given service exceeds its value, the organization should consider what the availability level should be. Service level management should consider such scenarios when working with end-users and customers in defining service level requirements.

6.5.2 Service level targets

After understanding what is required, the service level requirements, it is important to identify and develop targets that are meaningful and relevant. These targets need to be capable of demonstrating that the services that have been agreed to and that will be delivered are performing to an acceptable level.

Service level targets are defined as:

Frameworks	Service level targets definitions
Service Design	A commitment that is documented in a service level agreement. Service level targets are based on service level requirements, and are needed to ensure that the IT service is fit for purpose. Service level targets should be SMART and are usually based on KPIs.
MOF	Business-IT alignment SMF The following question is asked in the "define SLAs" activity of service level management: Does the service have an exact specification? Have the service targets (such as availability, capacity, and service hours) been agreed to?
ISO/IEC 20000-1:2005	ISO/IEC 20000-1:2005 doesn't define service level targets directly but does refer to them throughout the text. An example of this is provided as follows: ISO/IEC 20000-1:2005 specification. Service delivery process: (service level management) "The full range of services to be provided together with the corresponding service level targets and workload characteristics shall be agreed by the parties and recorded."

Frameworks	Service level targets definitions
USMBOK	Service management system elements A service requirement definition and management system to support the documentation of customer needs and wants, and translation into service guarantees. A service guarantee (service level objective) classification scheme, representing the most common types of service level targets offered by any service. The common types should include classifications that address support, performance, availability, monetary, and security considerations.

Table 6.5 Framework definitions of service level targets

Specific key targets generally form part of the overall service level agreement document. Service level targets should be identified and agreed between the service provider and the user of the service. Penalties may be applied to the service provider if underachieving on one or more service level targets in the form of service credits or financial penalties. Also it may have been agreed between the service provider and the customer that in order to demonstrate continual service improvement, certain or all service level targets may increase throughout the lifetime of the service level agreement. There are some considerations to be noted in regards to expecting the service provider to increase service level targets overtime to demonstrate continual service improvement.

Advantages
- Ensures that the service provider is serious about, and committed to, making service improvements.
- Encourages innovative thinking by service providers.
- If the right targets increase this could have a positive effect in increasing customer service and customer satisfaction.

Disadvantages
- Increasing targets alone will not ensure improvements can or will be achieved.
- Not understanding the current as-is or base-lining current levels of service may lead to inaccurate targets being set, or worse still setting targets that cannot be reached.
- Setting targets for the sake of setting targets without due consideration for both the organization, users and customers can have undesired results.

In situations where delivery of IT operations or a specific element of IT operations is outsourced, for example an outsourced service desk, it may be a requirement to increase the service level targets in order to demonstrate improvements and efficiencies that will be expected to be made over a specific period of time. One reason for this is that the outsourced managed service providers may want to try and differentiate themselves from their competition by showing their willingness and capability in improving service level targets throughout the time of their contract. Remember that improved service delivery (including improvements to service level targets) may be seen as a measure of success by the organization. However, paramount to this is that it may be recognized by the users and customers in regards to their perception of the quality of the service that they receive as perceived by them.

If service level targets increases have been agreed over the course of the service lifecycle, the service provider, or outsourced service provider, should develop a plan that aims to deliver these increases as early as possible. If left too late it may prove difficult to actually identify and understand how to increase performance and delivery in order to meet, or exceed the agreed increases in service delivery. Increasing targets may require the service provider to:

- change current working practices or develop new working practices
- identity specific areas where improvements can be made
- identify how to monitor, measure and report improvements
- initiate a program of change
- re-negotiate current contracts
- re-evaluate if the changes in the service level targets are actually achievable within the context of the current contract and subsequent underpinning contracts.

In order for service level targets to be relevant and effective they should be SMART:

- **S**pecific
- **M**easurable
- **A**ttainable
- **R**ealistic
- **T**imely

Specific

The target should be well defined, fit for purpose and fit for use. A specific target has an increased chance of being accomplished than a general target or goal.

The following questions help in setting a specific target:

- **Who** - Who is involved?
- **What** - What needs to be accomplished?
- **When** – When should it be accomplished? (Establish a time frame.)
- **Which** – Which requirements and constraints exist? (Identify requirements and constraints.)
- **Why** – Why does it need to be accomplished? (Identify the specific reasons, purpose or benefits of accomplishing the target.)

Measurable

Identify the criteria for measuring progress towards achieving the target. Identify that the target can actually be measured and if not identify what is needed in order for the target to be measured.

The following questions help in setting a measurable target:

- **Can** - Can it be measured?
- **How** - How will it be measured?

The ITSM library has published a book that discusses and includes IT metrics that are relevant for service management[10].

---

10   Brooks, Peter (2006). *Metrics for IT Service Management*. Van Haren Publishing. ISBN: 9789077212691.

Attainable

Validate that the target can be achieved either now or by the agreed time that the target is enforced. Base-lining provides an opportunity to compare current targets and target performance against any planned, change or future targets. Caution and good judgment should be exercised when new or changed targets are proposed that are radically different from what is currently being monitored, measured and reported on.

The following questions help in ascertaining if the target is attainable:
Can - Can the target be achieved? If not, then why not?
Has - Has a baseline been taken of the current situation?

If the target is not attainable, the question must be asked if it is realistic. The consequence of setting unrealistic targets can lead to management, user and customer dissatisfaction. Staff morale may decrease as their performance may be measured against targets that cannot be reached. Failure to baseline targets will affect analysis of the current *as-is* situation and the prospect of future trending as there will be no agreed measure to reference back to.

Realistic

In reality, setting targets that are actually realistic are generally proportionate to the investment made in the service, i.e. everyone may want or expect a 100% quality of service (QoS) but this comes at a cost. Organizations may choose to provide services with a reduced QoS but at a level at which is acceptable or bearable by the customer. All stakeholders should agree to realistic targets. It is also imperative that from the onset an exercise is carried out to actually understand the requirements of the organization and its users and customers. The organization will have to agree what level of service is actually needed to meet demand and should be able to base realistic targets from this.

The following questions help in ascertaining if the target is realistic:
What - What are realistic targets that can be set?
When - When is the service realistically expected to be available?
Has - Has the organization understood the expected demand of the service?

Should a specific target be measured? From all the possible targets, identify those that can and should be measured. The following table, while basic, can help with identifying potential service level targets.

Should it be measured?	Can it be measured?	Outcome
Yes	Yes	Service level target
Yes	No	Future service improvement opportunity
No	No	Do not measure

Table 6.6 Determine measureable targets

Service availability is often set to a target of 99.999% availability (the five nines). But this equates to approximately five minutes of service downtime or unavailability per year. For some organizations this is imperative. For others it is not. Remember, the more availability required, the more it is likely to cost in order to have that level of availability provided and guaranteed. If users and customers only use the service 8 hours a day Monday to Friday then is 99.999% availability required? By reducing the window of required availability to match that of the demand of the service, IT costs can be lowered, as well as any cost that is incurred by both users and customers. The availability window should be clearly identified and the availability target calculated against the availability window. Availability in this example refers to the availability of the service itself to the user, and not the availability of individual CIs or IT systems.

Timely
Targets should be established around a time frame. This provides a sense of urgency and a commitment that they will be created. Where there are multiple targets to be achieved, setting a time frame will facilitate the priority or sequence in which the targets are due to be achieved by.

The following questions help in setting a timely target:
When - When are the targets to be finalized and agreed?
What - What are the consequences of not agreeing targets on time?

6.5.3 Service level agreements
An organization needs to have guarantees and assurances in place in order to ensure that services are delivered as expected and as required. These guarantees need to cover both external service providers (for example vendors) and internal service providers (for example IT). A service provider needs to understand their boundaries of responsibility and the implications, if any, of failing to deliver their responsibilities.

For a service provider, over-delivering of a service may prove to be costly due to, for example, increased overheads, and unforeseen circumstance. Under-delivering a service may prove to be even more expensive due to, for example, penalties being imposed by the customer, assuming that penalty clauses exist and are enforced. So there is a fine balance to be maintained. However, over time customer and user demands may change, new markets open as old ones close, new technology becomes available as old technology is retired and therefore services and their corresponding service level agreements and service level targets must be continually reviewed and updated to meet these ever changing demands.

The following provides definitions of a **service level agreement**:

Frameworks	Service level agreement definitions
Service Design	An agreement between an IT service provider and a customer. The SLA describes the IT service, documents the service level targets, and specifies the responsibilities of the IT service provider and the customer. A single SLA may cover multiple IT services or multiple customers.
MOF	(Business-IT alignment SMF) A written agreement documenting the required levels of service. The SLA is agreed on by the IT service provider and the business, or by the IT service provider and a third-party provider. SLAs should list the metrics and measures that both sides use to define success.

Frameworks	Service level agreement definitions
ISO/IEC 20000-1:2005	ISO/IEC 20000-1:2005 specification. A service should be formally documented in a service level agreement (SLA). The SLA should be formally authorized by senior customer and service provider representatives. The SLA should be subject to change management, as is the service that it describes. The customer's business needs and budget should be the defining force for the content, structure and targets of the SLA. The targets, against which the delivered service should be measured, should be defined from a customer perspective. The SLA should include only an appropriate subset of the targets to focus attention on the most important aspects of the service. Note: too many targets can create confusion and lead to excessive overheads
USMBOK	USMBOK takes the approach that the service contract is also known as the service level agreement: Service contract The service contract, also known as a "service level agreement" or "SLA", is a customer focused and legally binding document prepared that explicitly defines the commitment the service organization is making to the customer. The service contract specifies in mutually acceptable terms the service levels, what the customers can expect from the service provider in terms of performance, quantities of work processed, availability and costs. It also specifies the level of usage and degree of cooperation the service organization can expect from the customer.

Table 6.7 Framework definitions of service level agreement

An SLA needs to be formally documented so that there is a written and signed agreement regarding the provision of services. SLAs generally relate to the provision of user and customer services. The creation of the SLA should include the service level manager, the service owner and people that can represent the business and customer needs. Some of the more common questions asked in regards to the SLA document itself are:
- What should be included in an SLA?
- Which details are relevant in an SLA?
- What does an SLA look like?
- Where can examples of an SLA be found?

Services differ from organization to organization as do service requirements. However there is a basic level of information that should be recorded in an SLA. SLA documents should be tailored to the organization, i.e. headers, footers and formats, fonts and layouts should be replicated where possible and formatting styles kept consistent to those currently being used within the organization. If service level requirements have been understood correctly and service level targets have been properly developed, the basic information for the SLA should be readily available.

A common issue that arises is the need for a standard SLA template. General thinking can lead to the question "why re-invent the wheel? If someone else has had the same need and has drafted and SLA document can their template now be used?" There is nothing wrong with this line of thought. However, there is no standard for an SLA template. There is no "one size fits all" template that should be used. Services differ, organizations differ, requirements differ and people differ.   *is this still the thinking circa 2015?*

ITIL Service Design provides an SLA template in Appendix F: "Sample SLA and OLA". Previously, the Service Delivery book provided an example of the details that should be included in an SLA in section 5.6: "SLA Contents and Key Targets". There are many examples of SLA documents

→ is this still current?

available that are quite easily found online. Instead of providing just another SLA template in this book, Appendix E Service level agreement contains a table that lists the most common content that can, and should be, included in an SLA. This approach allows an organization to easily incorporate these elements into their own documentation templates without enforcing a specific template format.

Depending on the organization and their circumstance, some items may be omitted and some items - while not listed - may need to be included. A fine balance is required. Including too few elements in the SLA may lead to confusion, a lack of clarity and a lack of responsibility. Include those elements that provide value in the understanding and delivery of the service and that will provide information that ensures the expected delivery of the service is maintained. If in doubt seek professional advice or guidance.

An SLA can exist internally or externally. Typical scenarios are presented in the following table.

Type	Parties		Example
Internal SLA	IT	Business Unit(s)	Payroll system. Corporate SLA i.e. an SLA agreed between the business and IT.
External SLA (as part of an underpinning contract)	Service provider	Customer (IT)	An outsourced managed service solution. For example service desk, hosting of IT systems or services

Table 6.8 Typical SLA scenarios

The external SLA referred to in the table forms part of the underpinning contract that is agreed between IT and the external service provider. If IT uses an external (outsourced) service provider to deliver a service on their behalf they need to agree terms and conditions within an underpinning contract to manage the specific costs and risks associated with the service. As part of the underpinning contract, an SLA will be agreed with the external service provider.

SLAs are important documents that should be agreed and signed. Therefore the documents should be under strict document management control. Some organizations excel at document management while others fall far short of the mark. Where formal document management control does not exist, an organization can place such documents under their change control process to manage any changes that are required to the document throughout the lifetime of the document. An option is to include the SLA as a CI and ensure that any changes and updates go through the change management process. Remember that changing the SLA document relates to changes being made to the service or the provision of the service and as such need to be managed accordingly by all parties. Changes to services should most definitely be logged as change requests and follow the change management process strictly.

Appropriate documentation should exist for each service and each service should be included in an appropriate service level agreement that has been documented, completed and signed. However the reality for countless organizations is that many services are in existence well before the service:
- is mapped to the required level, i.e. end-to-end
- is subject to an appropriate and adequate SLA

- has appropriate underpinning contracts in place that are documented, accessible, relevant, understood and linked directly to the service
- is fully understood end-to-end within the organization

Therefore many organizations find themselves in the situation of providing services or using services without having an SLA in place or with a poorly defined SLA in place. Worse still organizations may not even know what services they provide and rely on.

6.5.4 Operational level agreements (OLAs)

The OLA defines how the different departments in the organization will work together in order to ensure the provision of the service level requirements within the service level agreement. For example, how the service desk will interact with the various resolution and support teams.

An **OLA** is defined as:

Framework	OLA definitions
Service Design	An agreement between an IT service provider and another part of the same organization. An OLA supports the IT service provider's delivery of IT services to customers. The OLA defines the goods or services to be provided and the responsibilities of both parties. For example there could be an OLA: • between the IT service provider and a procurement department to obtain hardware in agreed times • between the service desk and a support group to provide incident resolution in agreed times
MOF	Business-IT alignment SMF An internal agreement between one or more IT teams that supports the requirements set forth in the service level agreements (SLAs).
ISO/IEC 20000-1:2005	ISO/IEC 20000:2005 specification Any existing UCs or OLAs must be revised during the design process. Everyone involved should be aware of any UC's or OLA's that apply to the provision of a specific service.
USMBOK	USMBOK takes the approach that the operations contract is also known as the operational level agreement: Operations Contract The operations contract, also known as an "operational level agreement", or "OLA", ensures the resources working within the service organization are aware and accountable for the role they perform in meeting the commitments made in a service contract. Operations contracts are a critical element of a governance framework. Ideally the team and group "charters", and performance measurement systems are linked to the achievement defined within the operations contracts.

Table 6.9 Framework definitions of operational level agreement (OLA)

An OLA is not the same thing as an SLA. They are both very different and serve different purposes. However they can be quite similar in structure and format. While the SLA provides guarantees and agreements regarding a service, an OLA provides an understanding of how the service will be provided by the IT organization. SLAs are written in language understood by the business and customers. OLAs generally contain more technical language. An OLA is an internal document applicable to departments in the organization.

OLA - internal; e.g, IT infrastructure
internal SLA - e.g, ERP type S/w apps

OLAs can be considered to be *back-to-back* agreements between the various internal departments within an organization. Therefore a small number of OLAs may exist that can cover many SLAs. An example of this is an OLA between the service desk and various support groups, for example level 2 and level 3 support groups. Such an OLA may detail how the service desk and these support groups work together and outline key responsibilities. For a service that requires user issues to be handled at some point by a service desk, the SLA for that service can reference an OLA between the service desk and various support groups. Refer back to the service portfolio pyramid that shows where the OLAs exist in the IT service catalog.

Service metrics may not form part of the OLA but will be included in the SLA associated with the service. However it may be worth creating a small number of key performance indicators (KPIs) in order to establish an indicator that the OLA is effective and that the teams and departments are working efficiently and effectively together. When considering KPIs, remember to report on what it is that matters most. However, ensure that the organization does not fall into the trap of reporting metrics for the sake of reporting metrics. It is imperative to identify a small number of key metrics to get started with. These metrics should be capable of reporting on key areas of the OLA and ensuring that the organization can understand the current situation. Too many reporting metrics become meaningless. Analysis paralysis is a common trap that organizations, or at least their various departments, can fall into.

An OLA can be very basic, for example detailing all the activities that are performed by the different IT teams in support of an IT service. It can include the hours of business for each support team and the expected availability of the IT service. Any differences between these hours need to be addressed as there will be a gap between actual support availability and expected support availability. This can be as simple as agreeing with the business that even though the expected availability exceeds the hours of support provided, the service will have no *out-of-hours support*. As long as this is accepted and agreed with the business, on behalf of the users and customers, this is quite valid.

At their most basic an OLA should detail:
* What is supported?
* What is excluded (i.e. not supported)?
* Who provides support?
* What support is provided at different levels?

As with SLAs, each OLA needs to be under strict change management and document management control and should be reviewed on a pre-defined and regular basis. Remember, the best place to store OLA and SLA documents are with the associated service records that they relate to. If they cannot be attached to the service records or if they need to be retained in another system, for example a document management system, then at the very least ensure that there is sufficient detail in the service record to direct someone easily to the documents. Placing a hyperlink (or similar functionality) to the document location can be very helpful.

It may take time to develop all the required OLAs and SLAs for all the different service types. Single SLA and OLA documents may cover multiple services, but this needs to be clearly defined and documented. However, it is necessary that these documents are completed, agreed, signed and attached to the relevant service catalog records. Otherwise there is no clear agreement between internal service providers and support teams (OLA's) nor a clear understanding of what has been agreed, or even expected, to be delivered in the case of services (SLA's).

6.5.5 Example of a service-focused service level management process

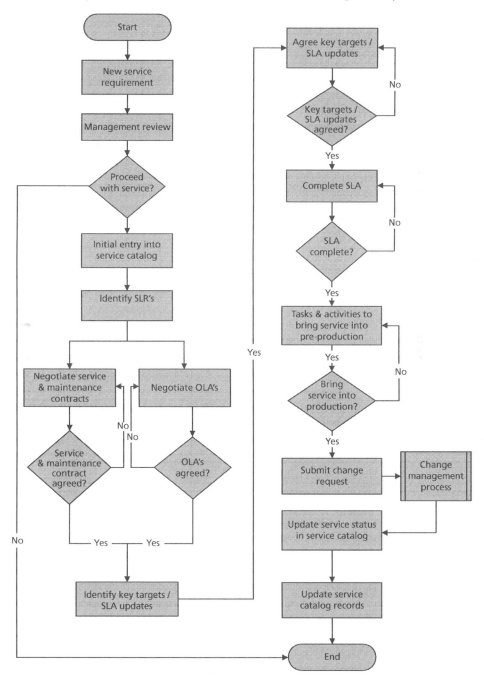

Figure 6.5 Example of a service focused service level management process

The process flow of figure 6.5 is an example of some of the main activities that are carried out within the service level management process which relate to the requirement for a new service. The aim of this book is not to create a complete service level management process, but to provide an example of a relevant process that provides activity steps that ensures service targets, underpinning contracts, service level agreements and operational level agreements are negotiated, agreed and documented. The end result should be that these documents will be recorded within the service catalog, related to the relevant service record and that they will facilitate required and expected business outcomes.

Input and outputs to other processes such as capacity, continuity and availability management, continual service improvement, monitoring and reporting have not be provided as they are outside the scope of this book but they are important elements that need to be considered within the utility and especially the warranty elements of a service.

Section 6.5 Service level management shows the sequence to be followed when defining service level requirements, service level targets and service level agreements.

6.6   Interfaces with ITIL or ITSM disciplines

Figure 6.6 represents the processes and functions that directly or indirectly interface with the service portfolio and service catalog according to ITIL. The service catalog and service portfolio do not, and should not, live in isolation from other processes, functions or even people. They will be equally ineffective if they are not integrated with the processes and functions that they exist to serve. Remember that processes, functions and people exist to provide business outcomes.

Many elements of the ITIL service lifecycle are represented in this diagram. Each process and function has specific responsibilities in regards to their inputs, activities and outputs. A common theme with these processes and functions is the relationship that they share with the service catalog. This relationship exists due to the interactions that each process and function has with the various services that exist throughout the organization and the role that they have to play in regards to these services.

ITIL is based on a "service lifecycle" and all the processes and functions in the five service lifecycle elements - in some way, shape or form - exist to support services from concept to retirement (cradle to grave). The key point to take away is that each process and function is linked in some way to the organization's services. Check all the organization's processes and functions to ensure that they refer to activities that support the organization's services. Ensure that processes interact with each other and that they are not working in isolation.

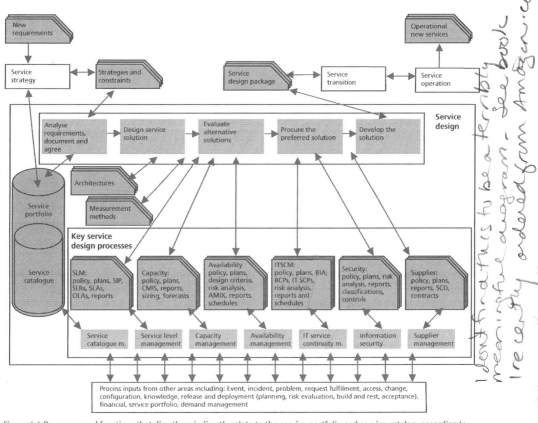

Figure 6.6 Processes and functions that directly or indirectly relate to the service portfolio and service catalog, according to ITIL (Source: OGC)

6.7 Ownership and roles

In order for processes and functions to be effective and serve their purpose clear lines of responsibility need to exist, are assigned and acknowledged. Failure to do this will lead to non accountability, a lack of responsibility and confusion over who is meant to do what. The following are applicable:

- each function and process should have specific roles defined
- each role should have clear responsibilities that allows the person assigned the role understand their obligations in regard to the role
- each role should be assigned to specific people to ensure that the role is carried out

The current version of ITIL introduced additional processes and functions that were not referenced in its predecessors. As a result of this, additional roles have also been introduced. On one hand it could be argued that ITIL has not invented these roles, that the majority of these roles had already existed in the past, perhaps under different names, and that ITIL has just structured them into its framework. On the other hand the reality may be that ITIL has created a multitude of roles to fit the increased processes and functions introduced in the current version.

Regardless, with respect to the service catalog there are a number of key roles that are important and that should be understood which will be highlighted in this chapter.

There should be an owner of the complete service portfolio at an executive level. This is to ensure overall accountability exists in the organization for the service portfolio. In order for this to be effective, ownership and accountability has to be delegated downwards to the various management layers in the form of:

- service catalog managers
- service owners
- process owners
- departmental managers
- operational managers
- line managers
- product managers

[handwritten note: → for NISPU NASP the service portfolio owner is MS Sapp (or one of the two deputies)]

The roles for each process and function should be identified, assigned to people and managed to ensure that they are carried out. Each process should have a specific owner. Some of the responsibilities of the process owner are to:

- represent the process and the delivery of the process outputs on behalf of the business
- ensure that a process exists and that it is fit for purpose and fit for use
- act as the overall champion and gatekeeper of the process
- ensure that the process is continually reviewed
- resolve conflicts that arise regarding the process
- ensure that relevant KPIs and metrics are identified, recorded and reported

This list of responsibilities serves as a guide and can be included in the process documents for reference.

6.7.1 Key roles

The following table is intended to outline a number of important roles that will be involved one way or another with the various service catalogs. The list provides a brief description of each role. The role descriptions are provided as an aid. They are neither exhaustive nor exclusive but offer a basic understanding of the roles. They can be added to the relevant process documents to aid in understanding what each role is tasked to do. This is to ensure the effective execution of the processes to which they apply.

In practice small and medium sized organizations may have to combine numerous roles as there is a considerable investment required in time and manpower in fulfilling all these roles. Even large organizations may want to combine some of the roles in an effort to lower overheads. Therefore, individual roles do not necessarily have to be performed by individual personnel but may be shared amongst a number of people. Equally, roles do not necessarily have to be performed by an individual person, for example supplier management may be performed by a specific team of people if the organization is large and is dealing with a high number of suppliers. The roles are not necessarily a person's single job but may only form part of their overall day to day job function or duties.

Some of these roles belong to processes and some to functions. ITIL can be somewhat unclear in what is defined as a process and what is defined as a function. Regardless, table 6.9 identifies some key roles that are required in regards to services and the service catalog. Additional roles can be obtained from the ITIL core books, USMBOK and similar bodies of knowledge.

At a minimum, the service portfolio requires the following roles to support its maintenance and upkeep:
- service portfolio owner
- service pipeline owner (service portfolio element)
- service catalog owner (service portfolio element)
- retired services owner (service portfolio element)
- service level manager
- service owners

Information about each role should include the:
- role name
- description of the role
- responsibilities required of each role
- basic level of skill and or/certification required (optional)

Role name	ITIL lifecycle	Role description
Service portfolio manager	-	There should be someone assigned as the owner of the service portfolio with overall responsibility for it on behalf of the organization. This would tend to be at executive level. Therefore the portfolio manager may be an IT executive who is not concerned with managing the details of each individual service. What this means, in practice, is that while the service elements that are in the pipeline or retirement are not formally within the catalog, they are in practice managed albeit separately from the service catalog management process. There can be individual managers assigned to each of the three elements that make up the service catalog, i.e. service pipeline catalog, service catalog and the retired services catalog. Equally there could be one overall owner of the three elements. A very important task of the service portfolio manager is to keep the service portfolio up-to-date to ensure that it provides value to the organization. In addition, keeping the service portfolio up-to-date determines if the service portfolio is seen as "valid and useful" to the organization. It should be recognized that, in general, a lot of effort can go into building the service portfolio yet maintaining it is often underestimated or even overlooked!

Role name	ITIL lifecycle	Role description
Supplier manager	Service Design	The supplier manager is responsible for ensuring that value for money is obtained from all suppliers and contracts involved in the provision of IT and business services. The supplier manager is involved in the following activities: • manage the suppliers and the services they provide • ensure that underpinning contracts are in place and aligned to business needs • monitor, measure, review and report the delivery of services by suppliers • manage and maintain relationships with suppliers • manage supplier performance The supplier manager will ensure that a central repository, supplier and contracts database (SCD), exists for storing supplier contracts and that supplier details and the contracts are maintained on a regular basis.
Contracts manager	-	The contracts manager can be involved in the negotiating of contracts and the management and subsequent re-negotiation of those contracts during their lifetime. The contracts manager should ensure that each contract document is version controlled and follows strict document management control.
Service level manager	Service Design	The service level manager is responsible for ensuring service level agreements are defined, agreed, recorded and managed. The service level manager plays a key role in negotiating service level agreements and in the monitoring and reporting of service levels achieved to ascertain if the agreed service level targets have been achieved. Responsibility also exists to ensure that operating level agreements and underpinning contracts exist and are aligned to customer and business requirements.
Service catalog manager	Service Design	The service catalog manager has responsibility for producing and maintaining the service catalog, ensuring that all information within the service catalog is accurate and up to date. Administration tasks may be delegated to the service catalog librarian(s). In the same way as the service portfolio manager, a very important task of the service catalog manager is to keep the service catalog up-to-date and to ensure that it provides value to the organization. In addition, keeping the service catalog up-to-date determines if it is seen as "valid and useful" to the organization. It should be recognized that, in general, a lot of effort can go into building the various service catalogs yet maintaining them is often underestimated or even overlooked!
Service catalog librarian	-	Assists the service catalog owner with keeping the service catalog up to date and may extend to keeping all the service portfolio elements updated also. This includes keeping all the service catalog attributes updated.

Role name	ITIL lifecycle	Role description
Finance manager	-	The finance manager (financial management) helps the organization to understand the cost of providing services both internally (to users) and externally (to customers). Some internal and external services may have to be absorbed as an "overhead" while others may be factored into costs that are then passed on to customers when buying products and services. To understand the true cost of IT and the provisioning of business (user) and customer services a full understanding of how services are built from the lowest level components, i.e. the CI level and technical systems right up to the actual customer services is required.
Service owner	Service Strategy	The service owner role is responsible to the users or customers for the initiation, transition and ongoing maintenance and support of a particular service. The service owner should work in conjunction with the service level manager to ensure that service levels can be monitored and measured and are still relevant. The service owner has accountability for the service on behalf of the organization and should work with the organization to identify opportunities for improvements or changes in requirements.
Process owner	Service Transition	A process owner is responsible for ensuring that the processes that they own and are responsible for is being performed according to the agreed and documented process and that it is meeting the aims of the process definition. A process owner can own more than one process at a time. However it is important to ensure that process owners do not have a conflict of interest. The process owner for incident management should not be the process owner for the change management process as well as there is a conflict of interest within these two processes.
Configuration manager	Service Transition	ITIL now includes the service asset and configuration management process (SACM) and the CMS. The responsibility of the configuration manager is far too vast to be covered in this section. The relevant responsibilities in regards to service catalogs include: • implements the configuration policy and standards • evaluates the CMDB/CMS • agrees scope of the service asset and configuration management process and of the configuration items to be controlled • assists in the auditing of the activities of configuration management and of the CMDB/CMS Service asset and configuration management records information about CIs required to deliver services, including a logical model that represents their relationships. This logical model could be designed into the CMDB and in effect creating the technical services catalog.
Configuration administrator/ librarian	Service Transition	The configuration administrator/librarian is the custodian and guardian of all master copies of software, assets and documentation CIs registered with asset and configuration management. They control the receipt, identification, storage and withdrawal of all supported CIs. The configuration administrator/librarian assists the configuration manager with keeping the CMDB/CMS up to date and may extend to help with keeping the service records that exist within the CMDB/CMS updated also.

Role name	ITIL lifecycle	Role description
Change manager	Service Transition	The change manager is responsible for the change management process. The change management process ensures that the following activities take place in order that change activity happens in a controlled manner: • record change • evaluate change • authorize change • prioritize change • plan change • test change • implement change • document change • review change Change management is a controlling process that spans the control of all the elements contained in the service portfolio pyramid. Transition planning activities will be required but any changes to existing services or the introduction or retirement of services should go through change management to ensure that the changes are planned and approved.
Capacity manager[11]	Service Design	Put simply, the capacity manager: • ensures that there is adequate IT capacity to meet required levels of service • identifies, with the service level manager, capacity requirements through discussions with the business users • understands the current usage of the infrastructure and IT services, and the maximum capacity of each component • forecasts future capacity requirements based on business plans, usage trends and sizing of new services In addition, the capacity manager plays an important role in the evaluation and acquisition of new technology and should be actively involved in the architecture of new services to agreed standards.
Availability manager	Service Design	Availability management is concerned with: • providing high levels of reliability, serviceability and availability of services to users and customers • ensuring that all existing services deliver the levels of availability agreed with the business in SLAs • ensuring that new services are designed to deliver the levels of availability required by the business
Communication specialist	-	A communication specialist is required to enable, plan and execute communication programs in regards to the service catalogs (roll-outs), new services that come on-line and services that are retired. Communicating effectively to the organization and customers can reduce issues arising and increase awareness of available services.

Table 6.10 Some key roles that are required in regards to the service catalog

11   Capacity and availability management are vital, but often overlooked, elements within the context of services. After all the light may be on (availability) but actually how bright is it (capacity)?

A RACI grid can be defined not only for these roles but for all the roles within the ITIL/IT Service Management disciplines as these roles will need to interface with the others managers, practitioners and staff involved in the other ITIL areas. This identifies who are:

- **R**esponsible
  - the person(s) that carries out the task to its completion
  - responsibility may be shared with others
- **A**ccountable
  - the person who is accountable overall for the task
  - the accountable person does not perform the task
- **C**onsulted
  - the person(s) or role(s) that must be consulted before a decision of final action
- **I**nformed
  - the person(s) or role(s) who must be informed after a decision or specific action has taken place

6.8 Service packages *Bundles*

At its most basic level a service package is a collection of two or more services that are put together or bundled together in order to offer a collection of services under one service name. This can include bundling:

- multiple IT systems bundled together into an IT service
- multiple IT services bundled together into a business service
- multiple business services bundled together into a customer service

An example of a service package is the *communication service* within the service catalog schematic example provided in section 5.7. This is a business service that includes a number of IT services bundled together, in this case the *instant messaging* and *email* services. If provided, it could also include IT services such as phone (land-line and mobile/cell), blackberry and remote connectivity services. Reasons for creating service packages will be explained in the following sections.

6.8.1 Maximizing economies of scale
Service packages or bundles can benefit from existing infrastructure that is already in place. There is no need to re-invent the wheel or create new infrastructure where existing infrastructure can be used, modified or updated to accommodate the service bundles. A key element in achieving this is an accurate and up to date IT service catalog and CMDB/CMS. In order to utilize existing infrastructure it is imperative to actually know what is currently in place and what the current capacity and availability of the infrastructure is.

6.8.2 Increase service offerings
Packaging services together allows an organization to offer more options and choice to both its users (internally) and its customers (externally). In turn this increases the value that is perceived by the users and customer of the overall service(s) offered. Providing additional value (value add) can be a big differentiator within the marketplace where comparative services exist and compete for the same business. Customer value is expanded on further in the section 2.2 "Utility and warranty".

6.8.3 Reduce service costs to users/customers

By packaging services together, maximizing economies of scale and utilizing existing services and infrastructure, it is quite possible that additional services can be provided to users and customers at lower costs than if the service components had to be built from new. Lower costs to users reduce the cost of doing business which can be passed on to customers or the organizations shareholders in the form of dividends. Lower costs to customers can promote an increase in the use of services generating additional revenue for the organization.

6.8.4 Control of risk or risk mitigation

Risk can be mitigated against by utilizing services and infrastructure that is already in place and working, and by also using the organizations supporting processes and procedures. By not reinventing the wheel for every service, an organization can utilize what is currently effective and working well. However, thread carefully where services and their supporting processes and procedures are not running as efficiently and effectively as they could and should be. Adding more and more services onto infrastructure that clearly cannot handle the new load is destined for failure. Something will eventually break. In addition using existing processes and procedures without reviewing them to see if they are adequate may lead to process related issues. The key is to do appropriate due diligence in order to identify what can be capitalized on and to identify areas that will not or cannot support the new services. Remember the importance of capacity management and availability management?

An organization has an existing website that offers customers the facility to purchase books online. The organization can add the ability, via additional services, that allows the customer to manage their account and log a support request online and also to chat with an online representative. The existing infrastructure is there as the website is already in place and the various technical elements that are needed in order to make this available to the customer are in place. However the additional services may require extra IT infrastructure and business services to be put in place in order to not only work, but to perform as expected. Remember, availability equates to the light being on and capacity equates to how bright the light is. In this example, the website and the extra services may be available via a menu but if there is not enough bandwidth available the services may be all but useable.

6.9 Cost recovery and charge back

Organizations now require IT infrastructure, applications, databases, hardware and software in order to do simple and basic business transactions. Cash register tills are no longer standalone machines but are now linked to complex enterprise resource planning (ERP) systems. Website services can connect customers to a business globally, 24 hours a day. A data entry clerk uses business services daily. They are oblivious to the fact that the business services that they use are built from IT services that run on IT systems that require IT infrastructure all to be in place in order for everything to work.

Organizations are looking to do more for less and IT is seen as the great enabler in order to achieve this goal. Higher employee productivity is expected along with cost reductions in doing business at the same time. Organizations needs, wants, requirements and demands increase while IT solutions become more complex. The one consistent thing is that organizations are providing more and more services to their customers and because of this they need more and more business and IT services to provide their customer services. However IT is not free. It comes at a cost. And that cost, one way or another, has to be provisioned by the organization. Typically there are initial project/set up costs, *capital expenditure*, and ongoing costs, *operational expenditure*. There will most likely be additional costs associated with regards to making major changes and updates to IT throughout its lifetime if it is to remain valid, strategically important for the business, fit for purpose and fit for use. Unless IT can recover these costs it may always be seen as an overhead to the organization, regardless of the value IT provides to the business and its actual strategic importance. Does this leave IT, or parts of it, open to potential outsourcing? If IT is not seen as a strategic and core asset but just as an additional overhead, the answer may be closer to "Yes". Therefore, the question that IT leaders should be asking is: "How does IT recover its costs from the organization?"

Charging is a mechanism used to recover costs. However, in order to charge the organization for the services that IT provides, IT needs to know what services it actually provides. If only there was a central repository that contained details of all the services that are in use throughout the organization and in use by the organizations customers. Well there is. The service catalog is this repository.

Note: the use of the phrase "central repository" is used as opposed to the service catalog being a single source or one database or an isolated spreadsheet.

Throughout this book services have been discussed at the customer, user and technical layer. This level of taxonomy allows an organization begin to understand the services and the service packages that are offered. It also helps represent the underlying technical services and systems that make up the business and customer services. Basically the service catalog helps bridge the business and technology worlds.

In regards to charging for services, any charge should be:
- fair
- effective
- understood and transparent

Charging can be applied both internally and/or externally and should look to cover both the direct and indirect costs associated with the provision of the service(s). Charging for services may be spread evenly across departments. This approach may be particularly useful if all the direct and indirect costs are unknown. On the other hand, charging may be on a demand basis, i.e. the more of the service that is used the more the user or customer pays for it. This comes into force in mature organizations where the direct and indirect costs of the services are known and can be applied adequately to service packages. Costs can also be re-covered by applying a markup on top of the direct and indirect costs and which in effect becomes a form of revenue. So now, not only can IT cover the costs of providing services to the organization and its customers, IT can produce revenue from the organization.

Description	Details
Fair	The charges that the organization applies internally for the provision of services should be applied in order to at least recover the costs associated with the provisioning those services. In order to maximize economies of scale, IT needs to try to utilize its resources to the best of their ability. Setting service charges too high and IT may be in danger of being outsourced for cheaper alternatives and options. Setting service charges too low and IT is in danger of exceeding allocated budgets or requiring additional funding in order to meet the ongoing operational costs and to include the ever changing needs of users and customers.
Effective	Service charges should generate revenue for IT to cover at least some, if not all, of the costs involved in the provision of goods and services to the business and include any additional markup that can be applied in a fair and equitable manner.
Understood and transparent	The charging mechanisms should be clear enough for the user (or business unit that will be charged) to understand what is being charged for and who will receive the bill, i.e. an employee has access to order a new laptop from the internal actionable service catalog. However, they may not know that their department will be cross-charged for the laptop. A best in class actionable service catalog should have business workflows built into it that require management approval before orders like this will be processed.

Table 6.11 Internal charging

Description	Details
Fair	The charges that the organization applies externally for the provision of services to its customers should be applied in order to a least recover the costs of provisioning those services. Economies of scale come into play. If enough people use the service, the cost per person can be low. If the opposite is true the cost of providing the service may be higher. Applying service charges too high and the organization may be in danger of losing customers. However the organization may have the extra capacity available that allows them to provide the service at no additional cost to the customer, at a lower cost than would be expected, or at a lower cost than their competitors. Setting service charges too low and the organization is in danger of having to fund the difference themselves.
Effective	Service charges should generate revenue for the business to cover at least some, if not all, all of the costs involved in the provision of goods and services to the customer. Customer services may be costed in such a way that the cost of all the overheads, including IT, is factored into the price of the service and include any additional markup that can be applied.
Understood and transparent	The charging mechanisms should be clear enough for the customer to understand what they are being charged for and how much they are being charged.

Table 6.12 External charging

Cost models are required in order to fully understand the full cost of delivering a service or services. Direct and indirect costs as well as overheads all contribute to the cost of services and need to be understood if the organization is to begin looking at service charging. These costs may be very complex to breakdown and understand and as such the scope of costing services and cost models is beyond the scope of this book[12].

---

12   For more information on charging and costing, please read Sottini, Maxime (2009). *IT Financial Management*. Van Haren Publishing. ISBN: 9789087535018.

7 Technology

This chapter discusses technology developments, options and considerations regarding service catalogs.

7.1 Developments

With the advent of the internet came e-commerce and a new way that customers could interact with organizations. Customers can avail of an organization's products and services quicker, faster and smarter than in the past. Lead times from order to delivery have been reduced. Technology has reduced the cost of doing business (than traditional routes to market) and thus such cost savings can be passed on to the customer.

It is extending the capability of an organization to provide more services electronically to their customers which allows for the customer to avail of improved service offerings. The success of e-business has meant that organizations now utilize more and more technology in order to deliver value to customers. These technologies allow businesses to reach customers quicker, smarter and faster and at lower cost than traditional methods and routes to market. Cost savings are enjoyed by organizations, and customers benefit from less of their time needed in their interactions with organizations. E-business has allowed organizations extend their offerings to new markets, new territories and new customers and to expand their product lines. E-business will help drive down the cost of actually doing business thus allowing organizations to pass on savings by way of lower prices to their customers. Equally, customers benefit from a wider product range, ease of use and lower prices, all available at the click of a mouse.

Within the IT space organizations can also avail of technology to allow their staff (users) to also work quicker, faster and smarter and to maximize their efficiencies and effectiveness. Chief information officers (CIOs) are mandated to reduce operational costs and to utilize IT as much as possible in this pursuit. Organizations have to exploit the use of Web 2.0, open source standards, application hosting and similar technologies and services. Platforms are extending the capability of the organization to provide more services electronically, not only to their customers, but also their staff which allows for the staff to avail of quicker and more efficient ways to do their job. This can reduce the cost of delivering business to the customer thus increasing saving made to both for the organization and customer.

7.1.1 Software as a Service

Service catalog applications are now being offered via Software as a Service (SaaS). SaaS allows suppliers to host service catalog applications, amongst others, on behalf of the organization whereby the organization, and their customers, will use the application on demand and as required. As the application is hosted by the supplier, there are no traditional initial upfront costs for hardware or software. Consultancy fees may apply especially if configuration of the software is required and perhaps setup costs also. The cost to the organization is usually rolled up into a service charge that is levied to the organization for using the service. This provides a predicable monthly, quarterly or yearly charge which is easier to manage from a budgeting perspective. Configuration of the service catalog should be possible though it is very important to check this out with the SaaS hosting company. It is not unknown for the hosting company to stipulate that no configuration changes can take place as this would affect the usability for other customers using the same service. Be sure to check beforehand that configuration changes can be made to meet the stakeholders, users and customer's requirements. The following table contains some basic advantages and disadvantages of using SaaS to the customer.

[handwritten margin note: Must his idea a caught on?]

Advantages	Details
Reduced costs	As the service is shared by other customers the overall traditional costs to the service provider should be lower and therefore can be passed on to their customers i.e. the organization that is looking for service catalog capabilities.
Reduced need for expertise	The service provider should be capable of providing the skills needed to set up and support the organization's service catalog.
Transfer of risk	The risks of ensuring that the service is provided and available is transferred from IT to the service catalog provider (hosting company).
Access to service catalog applications	SaaS provides an organization access to service catalog applications that they might not have been able to afford if they had to bear all the traditional costs associated with setting up and managing new service catalogs.
Disadvantages	**Details**
Lack of integration	Unless all the different service catalog types are provided by the same SaaS hosting company there will be difficulty in linking those that exist within the organization to those that are provided by SaaS.
Transfer of risk *[handwritten: SLA]*	The risks of ensuring that the service is provided and available is transferred from IT to the service provider. IT lose control over this by effectively outsourcing this to the SaaS service provider (hosting company).
Lack of choice *[handwritten: —lock-in]*	The organization may be locked into the SaaS provider for provision of core service catalog applications for the duration of the service contract.
Limited or no access to data after contract ends *[handwritten: why the longer term]*	Once the SaaS agreement has ended, will the organization be entitled to the information contained within the service catalogs? In some cases the information is not provided back to the customer unless stipulated quite clearly within the SaaS contract.
Interfacing issues with other service catalog	The SaaS provided service catalog may not interface directly, or at all, with existing service management systems, service catalog applications or CMS/CMDB. *[handwritten: (service requests)]*

Table 7.1 Basic advantage and disadvantages of SaaS interface *[handwritten: If provided as SaaS, how actionable is it?]*

7.1.2 Cloud computing

At a very basic level cloud computing is the concept of using the internet, commonly referred to as "the cloud", to allow people to access technology enabled services. Typically the underling IT infrastructure of the service provider using cloud computing is moving away from physical hardware to virtualized platforms housed in data centers. The IT infrastructure will need to be scalable and resilient enough to cope with demand, continuity, and security and so on. Managed service providers (MSP's) will be responsible for providing different elements of the services, or in some cases perhaps the entire spectrum of services, though mutual partnerships may be involved.

[handwritten margin note: optional — other categories]

Service packages, or bundles, as discussed in chapter 6.8 Service packages, will be used to gain competitive advantage and to differentiate one organization from next who are providing similar services.

Without going into a technical discussion on cloud computing as the scope of cloud computing is outside of this book, it should be evident that service providers who utilize cloud computing will need to be able to deal effectively with the following considerations shown in table 7.2:

Considerations	Suggested service catalog
Understand the services that they provide from a technical point of view.	IT service catalog
Manage and control the services.	Business service catalog Business actionable catalog Customer service catalog
Manage service providers and suppliers.	Supplier catalog Product catalog Professional services catalog
Translate these technical services into something that customers can use, understand and are willing to pay for.	Customer service catalog Customer actionable catalog

Table 7.2 Considerations

Therefore the service catalog, and the service portfolio, should be recognized as key strategic assets to be used by service providers operating within this space.

7.2 Technology considerations

There are many factors to consider when contemplating different technology options, solutions and repository types. Some of these have already been mentioned throughout the book while a number of the more important ones are presented below.

Organizations that try and develop a service catalog and look to the technology first to solve the problems of providing service catalog capabilities are taking the wrong approach. Organizations must first identify what it is that they want to achieve from the service catalog and understand how the users and customers of the service catalog will benefit from it and what business processes it is to support. Allowing the technology to dictate what the organization can do and achieve with the service catalog may not produce a service catalog that provides the functionality required by the organization. Some service catalog providers will be able to provide more functionality than others while some are more capable of being integrated with other IT and service management systems than others. Unfortunately some service catalog providers may claim to provide service catalog capabilities but the reality is that they do not, or may offer very limited service catalog functionality. Technology should be used to support the presentation, usability and automation of the service where possible and only where it makes sense to do so. The technology should be fit for purpose and fit for use, i.e. it should be capable of supporting and providing the actual requirements of the organization, users and customers.

Designing service offerings around technology capabilities alone will not provide for successful business outcomes. If technology is the sole focus in regards to providing services this could potentially lead to undesired, outputs and outcomes. Technology that is used on its own does not generally provide the desired solution. The bottom line is that technology enables outcomes. But technology can as easily disable outcomes if used incorrectly and if it is not aligned to business processes and outcomes. Granted, in this day and age organizations are looking to do more with IT for less in an effort to reduce costs. IT plays a part in enabling organizations to work more efficiently and cost effective. However, it should be evaluated whether using existing technology is going to save money in the long run:

* Is the expected outcome going to be delivered?
* Are manual tasks actually reduced or are more introduced?
* Are new bottlenecks introduced or existing ones eradicated?
* Is the service designed around what the technology can do as opposed to what is required by the organization?
* Does the overhead of supporting the technology increase with any bolt-on integrations?

For the organizations that are playing catch-up there are a number of considerations to take into account. The most fundamental of these considerations are:

* **Need** - Identify the need to develop a service portfolio.
* **Value** - Understand the value a service portfolio can provide to both the organization and its customers.
* **Priority** - Identify which service catalog types are needed first, IT service catalog, customer service catalog or actionable service catalogs.
* **Decision** - Make a decision whether to proceed, when to proceed and how to proceed.

Table 7.3 represents basic advantages and disadvantages regarding some of the different options available that can be used to represent the service catalog types. It must be noted that the very basic nature of spreadsheets and documents will prevent any reasonable level of maturity of the service catalog from ever being attained.

Repository type	Advantages	Disadvantages
Spreadsheet	<ul><li>cost of ownership reduced</li><li>small organizations can use</li><li>reduced admin overhead</li><li>filtering possible but basic</li><li>basic and less complex</li></ul>	<ul><li>is just a spreadsheet</li><li>not integrated with the CMS</li><li>limited access</li><li>administration is manual</li><li>limited functionality</li><li>does not support the actionable service catalog</li></ul>
Document	<ul><li>cost of ownership reduced</li><li>small organizations can use</li><li>reduces admin overhead</li><li>filtering not possible</li><li>basic and less complex</li></ul>	<ul><li>is just a static document</li><li>not integrated with the CMS</li><li>limited access</li><li>administration is manual</li><li>basic and less complex</li><li>does not support the actionable service catalogs</li></ul>

Repository type	Advantages	Disadvantages
Service catalog/ specialist software applications or CMDB/CMS	• increased flexibility • increased capability • scalable • may provide actionable service catalog capabilities • easy access • may support web interface • rich format • workflows automate processes	• cost of ownership increased • administration overhead increased • cost of licenses • ongoing support and maintenance costs • end-user training required • increased complexity • may take long time to complete to requirements specification
Software as a Service (SaaS)	• less expensive due to greater economies of scale • lower initial upfront capital costs. • predicable fixed costs • access to specialist service catalog applications • "tried and tested" by existing SaaS customers	• shared infrastructure • locked into one supplier • reliant on single supplier • may be difficult or expensive to customize • data ownership may be unclear, or worse retained by SaaS provider after contract end • uncertainty of how will services be provided after contract end

may be longer term lock-in

Table 7.3 Possible media types for various service catalogs

Configuration item information contained in the CMDB/CMS and their relationships can be used as a view that in effect provides an IT service catalog. If done correctly this can increase the value and benefit of the CMDB while removing the cost of having to purchase a separate system or application. Another direct benefit is that the organization does not have to duplicate the content of the CMDB/CMS. It can use the information already contained within the CMDB/CMS, which should also be controlled under change management. Generally some configuration of the CMDB will be required in order to effectively create an IT service catalog. Regardless of the repository type there are a number of crucial elements that apply to any service catalog type which will be discussed in the following section.

7.2.1 Costs and licensing

Some repository types, such as documents and spreadsheets, may not require any additional upfront costs provided that they are adequately licensed. However there is a trade off in this situation where there is limited and very basic functionality provided by these low cost options. Service catalog applications will generally require upfront capital costs for software, consultancy, IT infrastructure and so on. Another consideration applies to systems that provide more than just service catalog capabilities. More advanced systems can provide modules that support service management processes and additional capabilities. Each module, including the service catalogs may have to be licensed individually or in bundles. This has the advantage of allowing an organization to just license modules that they need and will use and obtain more functionality on an as-needed basis. It has a potential disadvantage in that organizations may find it difficult to get financial approval to license additional modules or functionality after the initial system or application has been installed, configured and put into production.

Understand the licensing requirements and licensing options with regards to any application that can provide service catalog capabilities. Most, if not all, applications require some form of license to be purchased before their service catalogs can be used. Exceptions may arise when the product used specifically provides service catalog functionality out-of-the-box as part of the basic application. It is important to understand the licensing requirements of service catalog applications in order to evaluate the costs of licensing the service catalog. While the software for a service catalog application may appear inexpensive to purchase, the licensing may increase the overall costs significantly. A number of licensing options should be available for access to the service catalog including:

- Fixed or named licenses can be more expensive on a license per license basis but guarantees access to the system for the accounts assigned to each named license.
- Concurrent or floating licenses can be a less expensive option but will limit logins to the service catalog to the amount of licenses available, even though more accounts can be created that licenses exist. This option may better suit actionable service catalogs where there is potential for a large number of users or customers requiring access, though not all at the same time.
- Free licenses may be provided for actionable service catalogs, where the license required is a license to use the actual service catalog module. This type of licensing is application specific though not always offered or available.

7.2.2 Interface   Gui

The service catalog interface is the mechanism by which the end-user or customer interacts with and uses the different service catalog types. It is critical that the interface is developed appropriately for the end-user or customer to use. The interface used to show service records and service record relationships may be different to that which presents the actionable service catalogs.

Key interface elements include:
- should be intuitive, easy to use and developed with the user in mind
- customer views may differ from business user views
- keep it simple but effective
- maximize potential up-sell opportunities for customers or additional functionality for end-users

7.2.3 Workflow

Workflow allows for the automation of a sequence of activities. It is a very powerful capability but its ability and effectiveness differs greatly between applications. Workflow engines provide the ability to automate manual tasks and activities. This requires that sufficient analysis is undertaken to identify and understand the specific workflows that are required and to identify how these workflows can be developed within the application. Utilizing workflows can:
- reduce processing errors
- decrease the time required to service requests
- assist those involved in the process to understand what they are meant to do
- ensure a consistent, reliable interaction
- ensure that the action taken is traceable and auditable (workflows can be used to write their activity into an action log)

7.2.4 Integration capability

It is highly likely that by the time an organization comes looking to implement a service catalog, they already have services in place and will generally have some form of IT support in place for those services, either in-house, outsourced or in some other form. If so, they may have some capability to provide different service catalog types.

Established organizations may well end up with a variety of applications that provide different service catalog type functionality. New, start-up organizations certainly have the opportunity to choose a single, individual application that can provide all the service catalog types and even support a full service portfolio (if they can find one). However, in general how likely is it that a start up organization will want to invest in such an application right from the start or has the required knowledge to know if they need one?

There is a good likelihood that organizations may have to "bolt together" various applications providing different service catalog types. There is also a good possibility that the service catalog types will have to be integrated with a service management system and a CMS. This requires that these systems and applications can interface with each other. Some systems and applications do this better than others. It should be identified as early as possible what type of external integration capability exists with the service catalog applications and the existing applications that are in place in the organization. The following sections details additional considerations that explain further requirements for different service catalog types. The information provided is not in pure technical language but can be used to translate the basic requirements into technical requirements.

7.3   To build or buy a service catalog

An organization will need applications or systems that are capable of providing the functionality required for each service catalog type. There are a number of general options available:

- **Buy** the required functionality.
- **Build** the required functionality.
- **Utilize** existing applications or systems.
- **Blend / combine** the different options.

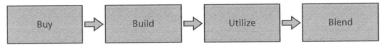

Figure 7.1 Buy, build, utilize or blend?

7.3.1   Buy

An organization may require a complete customer service catalog solution that is easily configurable and highly adaptable for its needs and is integrated with a service management system that can provide secure remote access capabilities.

The decision to buy a service catalog will require the organization to identify a vendor and product that is suitable for the needs of the organization. The organization should ensure that the vendor has the appropriate expertise in this field and that they can demonstrate this. Vendors may provide services that will scope, design and deliver the service catalog as well as offering to support the ongoing upkeep of the service catalog. Reasons to buy a service catalog solution include:

- gaining expertise and experience from specialists in the field
- requirements are specific and need specialized solutions
- automation and workflow capabilities that reduce manual tasks are necessary
- the cost of buying a solution is lower than that of the other options
- removes risk as others should have used the solution before (be sure to check with the supplier)
- there is more than one supplier to choose from
- there should be consultants and contractors available on the market, if needed (though check for smaller, lesser know solutions)
- the organization does not have to create the design specification and live with the consequences of omissions in design

Some considerations when buying a service catalog solution include:
- cost of the application
- cost of licensing the application
  - year on year
  - named vs. concurrent (fixed vs. floating licenses)
- cost of support and maintenance of the application (infrastructure, software, hardware)
- cost of initial install, setup and configuration (project costs)
- cost of future modifications, customizations
- cost of upgrading the application to a newer version in the future
- the possibility of the service catalog vendor being acquired by another company
- the possibility of the service catalog application being integrated into another application as part of a mergers/acquisitions strategy thus forcing an unexpected or unwanted upgrade or migration to the newer application
- availability of expertise within the market place
- ease of automation (provided that the application is easily configurable)
- the response and fix times agreed between the vendor and organization
- how well the service catalog application integrates with other service management solutions already in house
- supplier dependency

7.3.2 Build

An organization may not have the financial resources available to purchase an application or system. In addition, the ROI may not justify allocating money to fund such a purchase.

The decision to build a service catalog generally requires the organization to acquire the expertise by way of hiring people into the organization with the appropriate skills and expertise in this field or to use internal staff if they have the appropriate staff with the appropriate skills. Hiring specialist staff, even on a part time of fixed contract basis, equates to a higher ongoing cost by way of salary commitments and overheads when hiring staff into the organization or consultancy and/or contractor fess if using external personnel. Reasons to build a service catalog solution include:

- the organization has very specific and specialized functions that require a solution to be designed specifically for them
- lack of funds may necessitate the need to build the specific solution at a lower cost that purchasing it
- the IT organization may have existing bespoke applications and solutions that are not capable of integrating with available solutions

Some considerations when building a service catalog solution include:
- availability of expertise internally
- ability to integrate with existing service management tools, applications, systems
- ability to understand what a service catalog is, and is not
- ability to design a service catalog application that is fit for purpose, fit for use and tailored to the organizations requirements
- ability for the organization to support and maintain the service catalog
- locating suitable project personnel in order to deliver the service catalog
- business analysis capability to understand how services are built
- key people involved in the design, build and/or ongoing customization or maintenance leave the organization

7.3.3 Utilize

An organization may look to utilize existing capabilities.

Utilizing what is currently in place and available can be viewed as a potential cost effective option. However this may not always be the case as tradeoffs in requirements may be necessary. Reasons to utilize current capabilities include:
- lower cost due to utilizing current infrastructure and applications
- controls the IT footprint by not introducing a new application, platform or database that is not currently supported e.g. a service catalog solution may use an Oracle database but the organizations IT strategy is to only have and support SQL databases
- less disruption to the organization as they are familiar with the current systems and environment

Considerations include:
- Are the existing systems, platforms, services able to provide service catalog capabilities?
- What percentage of requirements can be provided versus what percentage of requirements are fundamental and cannot be left out?
- What will be the impact to current systems and services in terms of availability and capacity requirements?
- Will the cost of utilizing existing systems and capabilities exceed the cost and benefits offered from the *build* or *buy* options?
- Is the project likely to overrun and be over budget if it is managed and delivered internally?

An organization may utilize its CMDB to provide the IT service catalog. A basic IT service catalog can be easily produced by creating IT system records and linking them to the relevant CI records that make up the IT systems. Then create IT service records and link these to the relevant IT systems that make up the IT services. All this can be contained within a CMDB. The key factor here is the ability to create relationships and to define forward and reverse relationships.

7.3.4 Blend

An organization may provide an internal self-service option for staff to submit service requests and to log incidents. This "front-end" could be easily built using web based technology and integrated with the existing service management tool, i.e. by writing directly to its database, or using application API's where they exist, to create new service requests and incident records.

Organizations have the option to blend the options available that can provide the functionality required for the different service catalog types. Reasons to blend the available options include:

- increases the ability to provide a fully integrated solution
- increases the likelihood of delivering the requirements in diverse IT organizations
- allows the best use of IT assets

Considerations include:

- Multiple suppliers may be required to work together thus adequate project management is required.
- Complications may increase if there is a high diversification of technologies.
- Dependencies may exist where one supplier needs to finish work before another supplier can begin.

Before an organization looks at these options they need to undertake an exercise to understand the following:

- What type of services exist within the organization?
- What IT systems may underpin the delivery of these services?
- What is the target audience of the services?
- What are the services that will be offered internal and externally?
- What current capabilities can be used and exploited in order to deliver the actionable service catalog?
- Does the organization have the technical and business expertise required in order to build and develop a service catalog in house
- Is there a best fit service catalog application available on the market that can deliver the requirements of the organization and also interface and integrate with the organizations existing service management systems?
- Does the organization require, or will the organization require at some stage, an actionable service catalog?

Prohibitive factors may include:

- cost
- lack of integration between systems
- lack of open standards, or any standards

Reasons to consider before deciding to proceed with a service catalog initiative:
- insufficient stakeholder or management involvement, understanding or backing
- insufficient funds, no sponsor
- return on investment cannot be ascertained or is negligible
- value on investment is not realized, even for the most basic service catalog
- user and customer requirements cannot be determined, quantified or qualified

Reasons to keep things simple and examine the merits of creating the service catalog from existing infrastructure and technologies:
- organization has basic needs and basic user and customer requirements
- organization can utilize existing infrastructure and systems
- no revenue to be gained from the service catalog (for example internal service catalog), or more importantly little or no funding will be provided to produce the service catalog
- organization has skilled resources that can create an appropriate service catalog
- service catalog capabilities are present within existing systems, applications, service management tools

Reasons to examine the possibility of purchasing a service catalog application:
- requirements will require complex configurations
- workflow functionality required
- will contribute to revenue streams; for example a customer actionable catalog
- no existing infrastructure or systems to utilize
- funds are available to purchase a service catalog application
- ROI can be ascertained or is significant enough to justify the spend required
- market forces demand the need for one

Note: before the organization actually builds or buys an actionable service catalog it is very important to understand the processes that will be needed and to also try and develop these processes beforehand. An example of such a process is employee on-boarding for new hires into the organization.

This will require someone (or a team of people) to actually try and develop the end-to-end process flow of the service(s) that will be provided via the actionable service catalog. While these end-to-end processes do not need to be 100% complete for a proof of concept of prototype, they do need to detail the inputs, actions and outputs of each stage in the process. This will allow the organization test and see if the actionable service catalog being reviewed is fit for purpose and fit for use and is capable of actually supporting the requirements of the organization. Time after time organizations are left fitting processes around the limitations of tools and applications when in fact it should be the other way around. Tools and applications should be selected on the basis that they can support the requirements of the organization and in this case the organizations processes. Failure to "get it right" from the start can be a costly affair, yielding substandard results that may require further time, effort and money to correct in the future.

"Keeping it right" is very important which falls under the role of continual service improvement in the ongoing development, implementation and maintenance of any of the service catalog types. Continual service improvement also ensures that any changes in business requirements will be reflected within the people, process and technology aspects.

Epilogue

There is no doubt that the service catalog and the service portfolio are important strategic assets for an organization and key to helping IT align with the business, demonstrate strategic value and help drive the future success of the organization. Organizations are playing catch-up in regards to their adoption and use of the service catalogs and in understanding the strategic advantages that can be achieved from service catalogs that form part of an overall service portfolio.

ITIL is firmly focused on services and the service lifecycle. This is a welcome advancement from previous versions. In order to succeed at adopting, adapting and aligning any organization to this service lifecycle approach, a full understanding of services and the service catalog is required. The information provided in this book should act as much needed and welcomed guidance to users, practitioners, managers and most of all organizations. As stated earlier in the book, most service management frameworks advise that organizations should have a service catalog and all that goes with it, but do not provide specific details on how to achieve this. Books such as this one, as part of the ITSM library, are here to help bridge the gap between *saying* what good practice is and *accomplishing* good practice.

The book has purposely referenced leading ITSM frameworks and disciplines in order to help the reader understand what services are, what the service catalog is, and how they all fit together and provide value back to the organization and the users and customers that use these services. The majority of the time the definitions that have been used from these frameworks are similar to each other in what they describe. However, there still is no de-facto single definition of what a service is. Hopefully this book will help towards achieving an understanding of what constitutes a service and the service catalog in the absence of a single definition.

This book has hopefully filled the gap that exists in the public domain in regards to accomplishing a service orientated organization that is understood by the business, facilitated by-and-large by information technology that is aligned to helping the organization deliver value and fulfilling its customers' needs and requirements. It is unlikely that there will ever be a one size fits all type of service catalog or one solution that will provide for all different organizations and their needs. However, if the foundations are right there is every chance that what is built will stand the test of time. This book is about providing solid advice and guidance on the basics and foundations of what is commonly referred to as the *service catalog*.

By now it should be apparent that the service catalog is not an individual catalog or an individual entity but instead is a collection of different catalogs, made up of the basic service types. Each service type has its own distinct purpose, audience, design requirements, inputs, activities, and outputs that drive different business outcomes.

Larry English, a recognized authority in information management and information quality, stated the following in 2001 in DM Review Magazine:[13]

---

13   English, Larry (2001). "10 Years of Information Quality Advances: What Next?". *DM Review Magazine*. Feb 2001 "http://www.dmreview.com/issues/20010201/3009-1.html

"The mere use of any information technology will not succeed without the understanding of the paradigm of the information age and the principles of information management and process transformation. This conclusion calls us to find out why so many information systems have failed. We must understand the principles of the information age and transform how we manage the enterprise and information technology."

This is still quite valid today and very relevant in regards to the service catalog, the service portfolio and the topics discussed in this book. Looking ahead there will be an ever-increasing need for organizations to know and understand what services they need, and what services they provide in support of achieving business outcomes. In a world where costs continually need to be managed and reduced, yet improved service levels are expected, the need for the service portfolio and service catalog becomes quite evident.

As a final thought, to quote the maxim "You cannot manage what you do not measure". It is better to look at this a different way "You cannot *affect* what you do not manage". Manage the service catalog (and the service portfolio) well to ensure that the services used by the organization and its customers are providing the best possible value at the best possible cost achieving the best possible results.

Appendix A. Basic concepts for IT service management

A major aspect and benefit of ITIL is that it provides a common glossary and standard jargon that can be used across the IT service management industry. ITIL terminology is predominantly used in this book.

A.1 Good practice

Good practices such as ITIL, which have been adopted by many, can be used as a solid basis for organizations that want to improve their IT services. A good approach is to select widely available frameworks and/or standards, such as ITIL, COBIT, CMMI, PRINCE2 and ISO/IEC 20000-1:2005. All of these can be applied to many different real-life environments and situations. Training is also widely available, making it much easier to develop staff with the required knowledge and skills.

Proprietary knowledge is often claimed to be good practice, however it is often customized for the context and needs of a specific organization. Therefore, it may be difficult to adopt or replicate, particularly where multiple suppliers are involved, and therefore it may not be as effective in use.

A.2 Service

A service creates value for the customer. ITIL describes a service as follows:

> *A **service** is a means of delivering value to customers by facilitating outcomes the customers want to achieve without the ownership of specific costs or risks.*

Outcomes (or outputs) are made possible by the performance of tasks. They are often limited in what they can achieve by a number of constraints. Services enhance performance and can reduce the pressure of constraints. This increases the chances of the desired outcomes being realized.

ITIL V3 has the concept of a service portfolio and the service catalog. The service portfolio includes all services that are in development, in live use, or retired. The service catalog represents the services that are available to the customers.

A.3 Value

Value is the core of the ITIL service concept.

[handwritten margin note: Is this a typical distinction? I think Bill's charts assumed that everything in the Portfolio is in the catalog]

*From the customer's perspective **value** consists of two core components: **utility** and **warranty**. Utility is what the customer receives, and warranty is how it is provided.*

Another way of looking at this is to consider the following:[14]
- utility = fit for purpose. Does it meet the specification?
- warranty = fit for use. Will it perform; will it be available when required?

A.4 Service management

ITIL describes service management as follows:

__Service management__ is a set of specialized organizational capabilities for providing value to customers in the form of services.

A.5 Systems

ITIL describes the organizational structure concepts which proceed from system theory. The service lifecycle in ITIL is a system; however, a function, a process or an organization is a system as well. A definition of a system is the following.

*A **system** is a group of, interrelating, or interdependent components that form a unified whole, operating together for a common purpose.*

Feedback and *learning* are two key aspects in the performance of systems; they turn processes, functions and organizations into dynamic systems. Feedback can lead to learning and growth, not only within a process, but also within an organization in its entirety. Within a process, for instance, the feedback about the performance of one cycle is, in its turn, input for the next process cycle. Within organizations, there can be feedback between processes, functions and lifecycle phases. Behind this feedback is the common goal: attaining the customer's objectives.

A.6 Processes versus functions

The distinction between functions and processes is important in ITIL. So what exactly is a function?

*A **function** is a subdivision of an organization that is specialized in fulfilling a specified type of work, and is responsible for specific end results.*
Functions are independent subdivisions with capabilities and resources that are required for their performance and results. They have their own practices, and their own knowledge body.

Functions are often recognized as teams or groups, with a specific set of practices and tools. Section A.12 offers various examples of familiar functions in IT organizations.

---

14   The concepts utility and warranty are described in the ITIL book 'Service Strategy'.l

And what is a process?

> *A **process** is a sequence of interrelated or interacting activities designed to accomplish a defined objective in a measurable and repeatable manner, transforming inputs into outputs.*

Processes convert inputs to outputs, and ultimately into outcomes. They use measures to assist control and as feedback for self-improvement. Processes have the following characteristics:
- They are **measurable** because they are performance-oriented.
- They have specific results.
- They provide results to **customers or stakeholders**.
- They **respond to a specific event** - a process is indeed continual and iterative, but is always originating from a certain event.

Changing to a process based structure in an organization often shows that certain activities in the organization are uncoordinated, duplicated, neglected or unnecessary.

When arranging activities into processes, you should not use the existing allocation of tasks into an organizational structure as a basis. Instead, start with the **objective** of the process and the **relationships** with other processes. As the definition states, a process is a series of activities carried out to convert input into an output, and ultimately into an outcome; see the ITOCO model (Input-Throughput-Output-Control-Outcome) in figure A.1.

The **input** to a process describes the resources that are used and changed or consumed by the process. The **output** describes the immediate results of the process, while the **outcome** describes the long-term results of the process in terms of meaningful effect. **Control** activities are used to ensure that the process achieves the desired output and outcomes, and complies with **policies and standards.** Controls also regulate the input and the **throughput**, ensuring that the throughput or output parameters are compliant with these standards and policies.

These individual processes are built together into process chains. These show what inputs goes into the organization, and what the outputs and outcomes are. They also provide suitable monitoring points to check the quality of the products and services provided by the organization.

The standards for the output of each process must be defined, so that the complete **chain of processes** in the **process model** meets the corporate objective. If the output of a process meets the defined requirements, then the process is **effective** in transforming its input into its output. To be really effective, the outcome should be taken into consideration rather than focusing on the output. If the activities in the process are also carried out with the minimum required effort and cost, then the process is **efficient**. It is the task of process management to use **planning and control** to ensure that processes are executed in an effective and efficient way.

Each process can be studied separately to optimize its quality. The **process owner is** responsible for the process results. The **process manager** is responsible for the realization and structure of the process, and reports to the process owner. The **process operatives** are responsible for defined activities, and these activities are reported to the process manager.

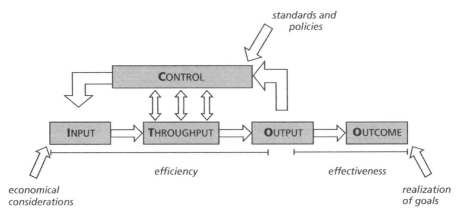

Figure A.1 Process diagram, based on the ITOCO-model[15]

Processes are composed of two kinds of activities: the activities to realize the goal (operational activities concerned with the throughput), and the activities to manage these (control activities). See figure A.1. The control activities make sure the operational activities (the workflow) are performed to time, in the right order, etc. (For example, in the processing of changes it is always ensured that a test is performed *before* a release is taken into production and not *afterwards*.)

According to the ITOCO model:
- processes have inputs and outputs
- they can be adjusted by means of feedback and comparison against standards
- they can be rendered more specific by conversion to procedures and work instructions
- various roles are distinguished in relation to processes (for example owner, manager, executor).

A.7   Process models

The **process model** is at least as important as the **processes** because processes must be deployed in the right relationships to achieve the desired effect of a process-focused approach. There are many different process models available. A master process architecture should be defined before individual processes are designed.

*A **process architecture** identifies the processes and process clusters, their interdependencies and interactions, their relationship to the IT organization structure, and the IT process-supporting application architecture.*

Organizations should use standard methodologies for creating process diagrams. In-house developed methodologies are often difficult to interpret in an unambiguous manner.

---

15   Source: Foundations of IT Service management, based on ITIL V3. Van Haren Publishing for itSMF International, 2008.

The business process modeling world offers various methods to create process diagrams, such as the unified modeling language (UML), the business process modeling notation (BPMN), and the business process execution language for web services (BPEL-WS). Other systems design approaches can be used to create process diagrams such as the CCTA/OGC SSADM or the USA DOD IDEF methods. Figures A.2 and A.3 are examples of the BPMN method.

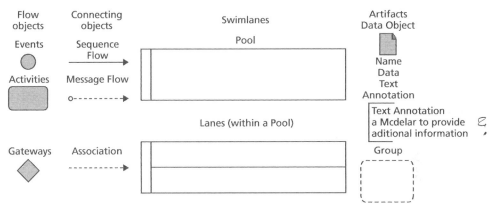

Figure A.2 BPMN elements

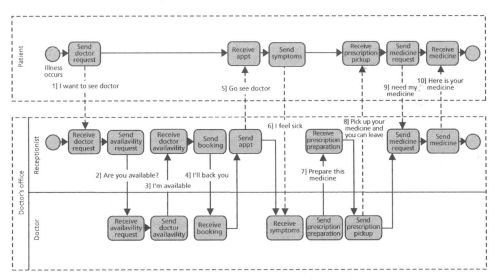

Figure A.3 Example of a BPMN process diagram

When described this way, it is easier to visualize and therefore manage a process. This is particularly true when processes are brought together in a process chain. Note that ITIL does not give much attention to creating these process chains.

An organization no longer stands out because of its unique IT management processes, but because of the extent to which these processes are truly controlled. It is therefore critical that organizations consider and build their own efficient process chains for IT service management, adopting and adapting the standard processes contained in available good practices.

In practice, there are many process models available in the form of supplier-based products. Unfortunately, the details of most of these models are not publicly available. This means that many organizations turn to developing their own based on the available non-proprietary schemas included in publicly available frameworks such as COBIT V4.1 and ITIL.

ISO/IEC 20000 clustering

ISO/IEC 20000 imposed clear clustering on its practices, see figure A.4. It is notable that the operations practices are out-of-scope in ISO/IEC 20000.

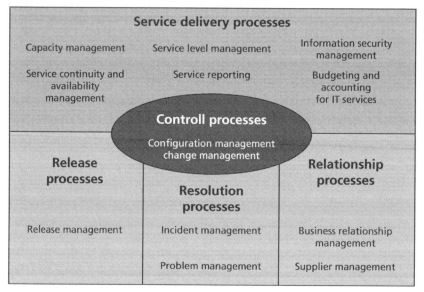

Figure A.4 Clustering of practices according to ISO/IEC 20000 *for IT Service mgmt*

ITIL lifecycle clustering

The lifecycle concept of ITIL consists of five phases in IT service management control. Each of these phases describes several practices ("processes"), functions and "miscellaneous activities". Many of these practices are applied across more than one lifecycle phase, see figure A.5.

Service Stategy	Service Design	Service Transition	Service Operation	Continual Service Improvement
demand management	service level management	change management	event management	7-step improvement process
financial management	service catalog management	service asset and configuration management	incident management	service reporting
service portfolio management	capacity management	knowledge management	request fulfillment problem management	service measurement
	availability management	transition planning and support	access management	
	IT service continuity management	service validation and testing	IT operations	
	Information security management	release and deployment management	monitoring and control	
	supplier management		service desk	
		evaluation		

Out of scope: business relationship management

Figure A.5 Clustering of practices according to ITIL

A.8   Processes, procedures and work instructions

The management of the organization can provide control over the quality of each process using data from the results of each process. In most cases, the relevant **performance indicators** and standards will already be agreed. The day-to-day control of the process is then left to the process manager. The process owner will assess the results based on a **report** of performance indicators against the agreed standard. Clear indicators enable a process owner to determine if the process is under control, and if implemented improvements have been successful.

Figure A.6 Process documentation in the ISO 9001 Quality Model[16]

---

16   Tricker, R.(2006). *ISO 9001:2000 The Quality Management Process*. Van Haren Publishing.

Processes are often described using **procedures** and **work instructions**, in accordance with the ISO 9001 quality management system model (figure A.6).

*A **procedure** is a specified way to carry out an activity or a process.*
A procedure describes the "how", and can also describe "who" carries the activities out. A procedure may include stages from different processes. A procedure can vary depending on the organization.
*A set of **work instructions** defines how one or more activities in a procedure should be carried out in detail, using technology or other resources.*

It can be difficult to determine whether something is a function or a process. A good example of a function is a service desk, a group of people executing the same set of processes, normally in the same department. A good example of a process is change management, where multiple people are involved who generally work for different departments. A practical guideline, based on ISO 9001, is to consider the contribution of people, process and technology to the subject. A process would only cover activities, a procedure would involve the people factor, and a work instruction would also involve the technology (see figure A.7).

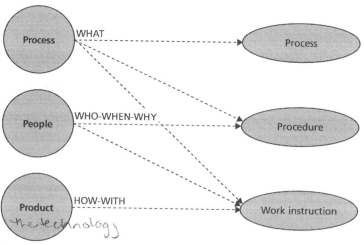

Figure A.7 Relations between the people-process-product paradigm and the ISO 9001 quality model[17]

In practice, it is not the process that instructs the people in an organization on a day-to-day basis, it is the procedure and the work instructions. Processes only show how the logic in a procedure is constructed, but they don't tell you who should do what, when and how. However, if you don't understand your processes and build your procedures from those processes, then procedures will often be inconsistent with related and interconnected procedures. Also, the reason for the design of a procedure will not be clear. This means that - before you can construct or improve a set of procedures that determine your effectiveness and efficiency - you must have your process system in place, and people must understand its basics.

---

17   Source: Hoving, W. and J. van Bon, 2008. *Functions and Processes in IT Management.* In: J. van Bon (ed.), IT Service Management Global Best Practices, Volume 1, pp 363-384. Van Haren Publishing.

A.9   Process and line management in a matrix organization

The hierarchical structure of functions can lead to the creation of "silos" in which each function is very self-oriented. This does not benefit the success of the organization as a whole. Processes run through the hierarchical structure of functions; functions often share some processes. This is how processes suppress the rise of functional silos, and help to ensure an improved coordination in between functions.

Organizations manage their activities from two perspectives: **process management** and **line management**. An organization using process management structures its activities in a neat series of processes, so that "floating" or "un-attached" activities are eliminated. This way, the structure of the organization enforces the need to follow the processes. And since processes are generally accepted as the efficient and effective way to organize activities, this will support the organization's performance.

An organization using line management will also manage their activities in organizational structures: teams, departments, sections, business units. These structures are normally ordered along some kind of hierarchy. This way, the organization makes sure that it is clear how activities are allocated to organizational responsibilities.

If an activity is sufficiently important, it can be managed as part of one of the defined processes, or it can be managed from the organizational line. It is possible, and increasingly common, for activities to be managed using both of these perspectives, creating the **matrix organization**. It is important to establish to which extent an activity is managed from the process perspective and/or from the line perspective. Figure A.8 illustrates the process management matrix, demonstrating how staff can be managed from different perspectives. Each individual organization can vary the extent to which it uses these two control mechanisms according to its own preferences.

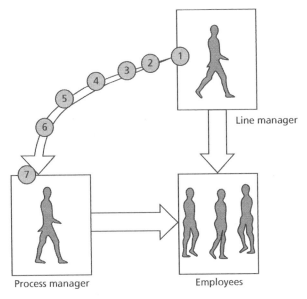

Figure A.8 The process management matrix[18] (PMM)

---

18   Source: IT Service Management – Global Best Practices, Volume 1 (2008). W. oving & J. van Bon, *The Process Manage-ment Matrix*, pp 309-323. Van Haren Publishing.

According to the process management matrix (PMM), the mix of the two "pure" control models can be described in seven positions:

1. **The pure line organization** - often represented as the familiar rake or tree structure. All responsibilities are cascaded from the top down; interconnections between different lines are not recognized. The line manager is responsible for controlling their team, which consists of staff or other line managers. The performance of the organization is the sum of the performance of the departments. As such, the department's result is a direct responsibility of the department managers.

2. **The line organization recognizes some processes** - In terms of control, this organization is still a pure line organization. One characteristic of this variant is that it recognizes patterns in the activities of different departments that lead to positive results. By laying down these patterns in a process description, it determines which activities must be executed, their order, and the quality criteria with which they must comply. The recognized processes are often cross-departmental. In this variant, the management of the department executing the activity and the staff involved bear exclusive responsibility for correct communication and collaboration.

3. **Tactical process management** - In this variant, the organization not only recognizes process-based relationships in the activities that it executes. In addition to variant two, it also decides to make someone responsible for the creation, maintenance, and reporting for the process. A key feature of this variant is that someone is appointed to this position of **process owner**. They own the process description and the manner in which the process is executed. As a result, the line management is no longer exclusively responsible for the control and results of the organization. The added value of the correct execution of well-structured processes and the negative consequences of their failure must be demonstrated not only by the process setup, but also - and especially - from the reports.

4. **Operational process control** - In this variant the process management, in addition to the responsibilities from variant three, is also tasked to monitor the correct execution of the defined process setup. In this case, "correct" means that the process is executed according to the process description, and within the constraints of the agreement with the customer. "Monitoring", however, does not mean correcting the execution, but detecting deviations and, if necessary, escalating this information. This means that the process management must be aware of the manner in which process activities are executed. It must also report (possible) deviations from the prescribed operating method or SLAs to the stakeholders, and inform them of the situation.

5. **Operational process direction** - Sometimes the organization may decide to strengthen process control by granting the process management a mandate of direction. The main characteristic of this variant is the transition in who decides and who escalates. In variant four, the staff or manager decides whether he will follow the suggestion of the process management. If the process management does not agree with the choice, it must decide whether it wishes to involve higher levels of the organization in the conflict or will accept the decision made.

6. **Operational and content direction** - While less obvious, it is possible to *also* authorize process management to decide which department - and which persons in that department - must execute activities. As a result, process management is allowed to influence content-related aspects. The process management selects the most suitable department and staff member in view of the situation. In this variant, the line management's role is virtually reduced to *resource*

management. The line manager must ensure that the department has adequate resources with sufficient knowledge to execute the activities. In this variant, process management decides on deployment of the resources.

7. **Full process direction** - This is primarily a theoretical variant. It is the last step in allocating more responsibility to process management. This variant allocates the responsibility for resource management to process management. The result is 'process departments', meaning that all activities that must be executed for a process are executed by resources from those departments. In fact, it returns the organization to the start because it boils down to full management along one single dimension, just like the pure line management in the first variant.

For an employee, it is important to understand how these "competing" management forces are balanced, to prevent conflicts in the prioritization of tasks. This problem grows even more severe if the same employee is also directed from a third perspective: **project management**. In PMM it is highly recommended that project management follows the balance of line and process management, running projects "over these lines" instead of adding another competing perspective.

A.10 Process and maturity

There are two mainstream "schools" of maturity thinking. They are based on different interpretations of the term "maturity":

- **Capability maturity** - explaining how well certain activities are performed, in a technical sense. Examples are CMMI, SPICE, the test process maturity model, the project effectiveness maturity model (PEMM), Luftman's business-IT alignment model, and Nolan's growth model. Basically, all of these models describe process capability levels, expressing how well processes are performed.
- **Value chain maturity** - explain how well an organization is able to contribute to a value chain. A value chain maturity model is shown in figure A.11 and examples of this school are the KPMG world class IT maturity model and the INK management model (based on EFQM).

Combinations can also be found, for example in the Gartner Networking Maturity Model.

According to the quality model of EFQM (European Foundation for Quality Management, see figure A.9), the road to "total quality" passes through the phases *product-focused, process-focused, system-focused, chain-focused,* and *total quality-focused* ("utopia"). This means that, before being able to realize a state of continuous improvement, the organization must first have control over a number of aspects. The phase in which the organization becomes skilled in managing *processes* is crucial in the maturity approach. The organization cannot focus on systems and chains until these processes are under control.

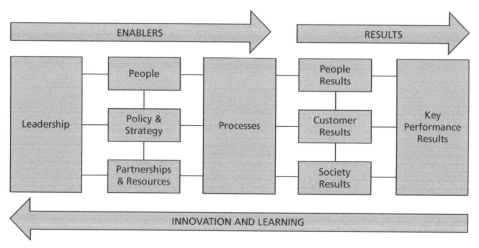

Figure A.9 The EFQM Quality Model[19]

The CMMI model (figure A.10) also deals with the extent to which organizations control their processes. The continuous representation, for instance, is expressed through the stages *incomplete process*, *performed process*, *managed process*, *defined process*, *quantitatively managed process* and *optimizing process*. The CMMI staged representation also defines maturity in terms of the extent to which the organization controls its processes.

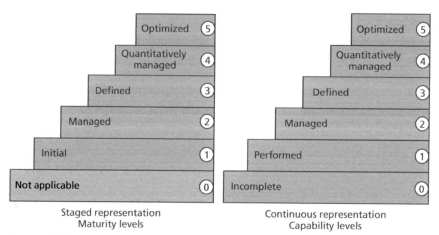

Staged representation
Maturity levels

Continuous representation
Capability levels

Figure A.10 CMMI, a maturity model for process management[20]

Processes are *internal* affairs for the IT service provider. An organization that is still trying to gain control of its processes therefore has an **internal focus**. Organizations that focus on gaining control over their systems in order to provide services, are also still internally focused. The organization is not ready for an **external focus** until it controls its services and is able to vary them on request. This external focus is required to evolve into that desirable customer-focused organization. This is expressed in the value chain maturity model (figure A.11).

---

19   The EFQM Excellence Model is a registered trademark of EFQM.
20   Capability Maturity Model and CMMI are registered in the U.S. Patent and Trademark Office by Carnegie Mellon University

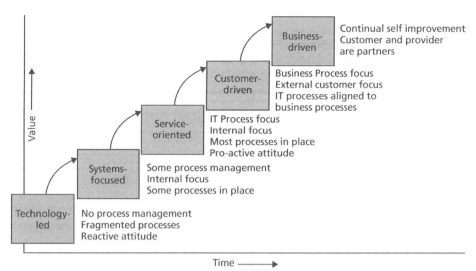

Figure A.11 Maturity in the value chain[21]

Because organizations can be in different stages of maturity, IT managers require a broad orientation in their discipline. Many organizations are now working on the introduction of a process-focused or still have to start working on this. Process control is a vital step on the road towards a mature **service-oriented** and – ultimately - **customer-driven** organization.

In the last twenty years, ITIL has made an important contribution to the organization of that process-focused approach. The development started in North-Western Europe and has made progress on most other continents in the last decade. On a global scale and in hard figures, however, only a minimal number of organizations have actually started with this approach - and an even smaller number have made serious progress at this point. The organizational change projects that were thought to be necessary to convert to a process-focused organization were not all entirely successful. The majority of organizations in the world clearly require access to good information and best practices concerning the **business processes of IT organizations**. Fortunately, that information is abundant. The previous ITIL books provided comprehensive documentation on the most important processes, and ITIL now adds even more information.

A.11 Core processes of a service provider

ITIL acknowledges the difference between functions and processes: functions (organizational capabilities) make use of processes (repeatable strings of activities). In ITIL, the description of such functions may cover *activities* that are not covered in the description of the relevant processes.   *so need to look at both fxn and process descriptions*

21   Bosselaers, Theo, Mark Griep, Joost Dudok van Heel, Joachim Vandecasteele and Rob Weerts (2000). *The Future of the IT Organization*. In: J. van Bon (ed.), World Class IT Service Management Guide (2000). The Hague: ten Hagen & Stam Publishers.

As explained previously, what ITIL calls a process does not always follow the above mentioned definition of what a process is. One solution to this is to consider the twenty-six ITIL "processes" as twenty-six ITIL practices. For example, in ITIL Capacity management covers a range of activities that cannot be ordered as a logical and repeatable sequence of activities. As such, the ITIL context describes a capacity management practice (CMP) or function rather than a capacity management process.

By definition, the structure of a process is in fact a series of activities that are placed in a logical order: a **workflow**. This workflow is controlled by means of the **control activities**. These control activities make sure the operational activities are performed in time, in the right order, etc. (for example in the change management process it is always made sure that a test is performed *before* a release is put into production and not *afterwards*).

Like any other kind of service organization, an IT service provider has only a very limited set of **frequently repeated basic processes** or process groups:
- Four processes are concerned with **effectiveness**:
  a. **Agreeing** with the customer what you will deliver (*contract management*).
  b. **Delivering** what you have agreed (*operations management*).
  c. **Repairing** anything that goes wrong (*incident management*).
  d. **Changing** your service if this is required by the customer or by yourself (*change management*).
- Two processes are concerned with **efficiency**:
  e. **Knowing** what you use to deliver your service with (*configuration management*).
  f. **Adjusting** (to) conditions that may prevent you to deliver tomorrow what you have agreed today, proactively eliminating risks that would prevent this (*risk management*).

This goes not only for an IT service provider, but for other service management fields as well. Imagine a catering service provider, the national post, or any other service provider: they all will perform these same basic tactical and operational processes.

For an IT organization:
- **Contract management** will cover areas of responsibility such as service level management, supplier management, business relationship management.
- **Operations management** will cover the activities required to realize the operation of the IT service, when the service is not down or changed. This would normally cover the planning and execution of all operations activities, including the monitoring of all services and components, which is the bulk of the IT provider's activities.
- **Incident management** covers anything that needs to be done for the repair of services or components.
- **Change management** covers anything to be done for actually changing an IT service or component.
- **Configuration management** covers all activities for providing accurate information on all infrastructure components which the organization uses to deliver their services.
- **Risk management** covers all proactive management activities that make sure that the organization will be able to deliver all quality of service (QoS) parameters that were agreed with the customer (in terms of capacity, performance, finance, etc.), while conditions are continuously changing.

Of course, an IT organization will have some kind of **strategic process** above this list. However, strategic activities do not usually get caught in process descriptions. First of all, the frequency of these activities is relatively low, so the short term repetitive nature is missing. And second, C-level managers (CEO, CFO, CIO, etc.) in strategic positions do not usually consider their activities as being standard and commoditized. The Service Strategy book in ITIL is a good example: although many activities are described, you will not find a strategic process in the book (according to ITIL's definition of process). The set of *high frequency basic processes* is therefore limited to the tactical and operational level, and covers no more than six core processes.

A.12 Setting up functions in the service provider's organization

Looking at the provider's organization, and at documented best practices, we can recognize a large number of functions. Each of these functions uses one or more of the core processes. Functions can have different formats, including:

- **Infrastructure format** – focused on managing a part of the information system: for example the application, the network, the database, desktops, servers, mainframes, telephony, database, data, system software, middleware, power, air conditioning and humidity, and so forth. Examples of well-known functions are application management (team), network management (team), database administration (team?)
- **Service quality format** – focused on managing a quality aspect, for example availability, continuity, security. Relevant functions can be availability management (team), IT service continuity management (team), security management (team).
- **Activity format** - focused on managing one or more specific activities (processes). Relevant functions can be change management team, configuration management team, requirements engineering, service desk.
- **Organizational format** – focused on organizing responsibilities in departments according to criteria such as size, region, skills, specialty. Examples of functions can be the EMEA Business Unit, Team West, Corporate Headquarters.

A function can of course also be a mix of any of these - and other - formats. Finding the optimum organizational structure is a balancing act: which functions are most important to the organization, which processes are essential, how is management along the function dimension (also known as "the line") and along the process dimension balanced?

You may now recognize the following examples of regular functions:
- **Capacity management** is an *infrastructure function* that uses a set of basic processes:
  - for realization of the capacity of the agreed services at the agreed rate/demand, this function uses *operations management*
  - for repairing capacity issues it uses *incident management*
  - for changing capacities it uses *change management*
  - for agreeing on capacity aspects it uses *contract management*
  - for proactive actions concerning capacity issues it uses *risk management process*
  - for the knowledge of which capacity carriers are deployed in which parts of the enterprise infrastructure it uses *configuration management*

- **Security management** is a *service quality function* that uses a set of basic processes:
  - for realization of the security of the agreed services at the agreed rate/demand, this function uses *operations management*
  - for repairing security issues it uses *incident management*
  - for changing security it uses *change management*
  - for agreeing on security aspects it uses *contract management*
  - for proactive actions concerning security issues it uses *risk management*
  - for the knowledge of which security measures are deployed in which parts of the enterprise infrastructure it uses *configuration management*
- **Service desk** is an *activity function* (call handling) that uses a set of basic processes:
  - for the operational support of calls (service requests) according to the agreed services at the agreed rate/demand, this function uses *operations management*
  - for handling incident calls it uses *incident management*
  - for handling change calls it uses *change management*
  - for agreeing on call handling performance it uses *contract management*
  - for proactive actions of call handling issues it uses *risk management*
  - for the knowledge of which service infrastructures are deployed in which parts of the enterprise it uses *configuration management*
- **Corporate Headquarters** is an *organizational function* that uses a set of basic processes:
  - for realization of the agreed services at the agreed rate/demand, this function uses *operations management*
  - for repairing service issues it uses *incident management*
  - for changing services it uses *change management*
  - for agreeing on service levels it uses *contract management*
  - for proactive actions on service issues it uses *risk management*
  - for the knowledge of which service infrastructures are deployed in which parts of the enterprise it uses *configuration management*
- Network management, application management, data management, financial management, workload management, print management, knowledge management, and so forth, will now all be recognized as variations to the themes above.

If these functions would be perceived as processes, this would require descriptions in terms of logical sequences of activities, inputs and outputs, feedback mechanisms, et cetera. The fact is that the functions listed above are not normally described in those terms, and that thus the interpretation as a function is more realistic than the interpretation as a process.

The number of functions that can be defined is endless: a function can be defined on each service attribute that is agreed upon. Common paragraphs in an SLA deal with familiar QoS's such as availability, capacity, cost and continuity. As a consequence, we will find availability management, capacity management, financial management and continuity management functions in that organization. But if the organization also agreed to QoS's for performance, reliability, maintainability, scalability or others - you may expect to find functions such as performance management, reliability management, maintainability management, scalability management and others. These functions would then all use the six basic processes for their activities.

Appendix B. Example - A Visit to the doctor

During the writing of this book I found myself sitting in the doctor's surgery waiting for my appointment. On a wallboard was a list of the services available at the surgery. As I looked at this list of services it hit me and I made the connection. I was looking at the customer view of the service catalog for the clinic. It had the characteristics of a *customer service catalog* as it:
— is published to customers
— is presented in customer language
— represents the services that the customer can order, consume or use
— provides details of how the customers could use the services, for example booking details, and phone numbers were provided

During the visit the doctor used a computer system in order to access my file and print my prescription for medication. The receptionist processed each patient's visits using a booking system, accessed the clinic's email account, printed receipts and used a credit card terminal to process patient payments. All these would be considered business services. They are used by the business (the clinic) to support delivering the customer services, i.e. the list of services on the wallboard. These had the traits of a *business service as they*:
— are services used in the organization to support business processes
— consist of one or more IT services that enable a business process or function
— are services used by the business to support the business outcomes
— can allow for charging to be applied to the business services
— are seen from the perspective of the business
— deliver value to the business

The users of these business services (the staff) do not necessarily understand, or have to understand, the IT working behind the scenes. They don't need to. They just need the IT systems and IT services to work as expected. I asked what the receptionist would do if the email didn't work, if the patient information system had a problem or if credit card terminal had a problem and was informed that there is a support number for the receptionist to use to report problems. The clinic is a franchise and so had a number of other clinics throughout the country. They all call the same number to get help if they experience issues with the IT services. This central point of contact represents a service desk. It is at the service desk where IT services, IT systems and CIs come to the forefront. The service desk and support teams that they will escalate to need to be able to relate the business services to the IT services and IT systems that are required to provide them. This is where the business service catalog and the IT service catalog are used. In order to diagnose problems these catalogs can be used to help understand how the services are built and to access information that is available about the services. I also found out that I can book a doctor or dentist appointment from their website. This facility is their equivalent to an actionable service catalog that is provided to the customer.

Recently the same clinic has announced that "Flu and Pneumococcal vaccines will now be available at all locations". This is obviously due to the demand for this service, or is a service that is seen as something that can contribute to revenue growth. Either way it is a new customer service that will require business services for it to be delivered, which is most likely being provided due to customer demand.

Figure B.1 shows the main page from the web site[22] of the medical centre mentioned previously. It is an example of a customer service catalog and a customer actionable catalog together. This demonstrates that the two can co-exist. It also demonstrates the value-add that an actionable service catalog can provide alongside a customer service catalog. It should be noted that this organization is not selling products directly to customers through this particular website, but services. Therefore this example does not represent a product catalog.

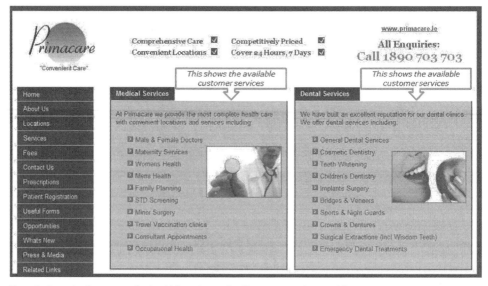

Figure B.1 Example of a customer (actionable) service catalog (Source: www.primacare.ie)

The "Provide Feedback" option in figure B.2 allows the customer to interact with the organization. This can be achieved simply, requires little workflow, for example a basic "mailto:" will suffice. It can also be used to create an automated "service request", categorized as feedback, and assign the record to the service desk. The majority of service desk applications will provide functionality that can create an automatic record or service request from an email or to use in built functionality, for example an API to achieve this.

---

22   Primacare, *http://www.primacare.ie/*, Primacare Group 2009.

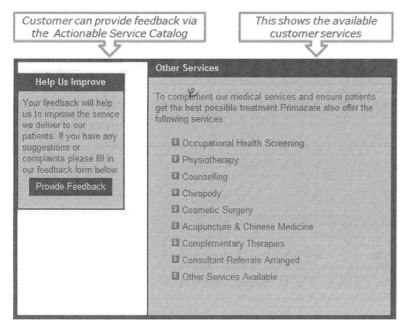

Figure B.2 Example of feedback service (Source www.primacare.ie)

The option shown in figure B.3 allows the customer to request a service, i.e. an appointment or a callback. The minimum amount of information is requested. This makes it:

- easy for the customer to complete
- quick for the customer to complete
- minimizes errors

Also, the organization has included a check box option that allows the customer to be "contacted by email with information or offers". This is an excellent marketing strategy with very low cost. It can also be seen by the user as a value added service. The key to success with this "service" is:

- keep the content relevant
- don't overuse it
- confidentiality - don't provide the customers details to a third party

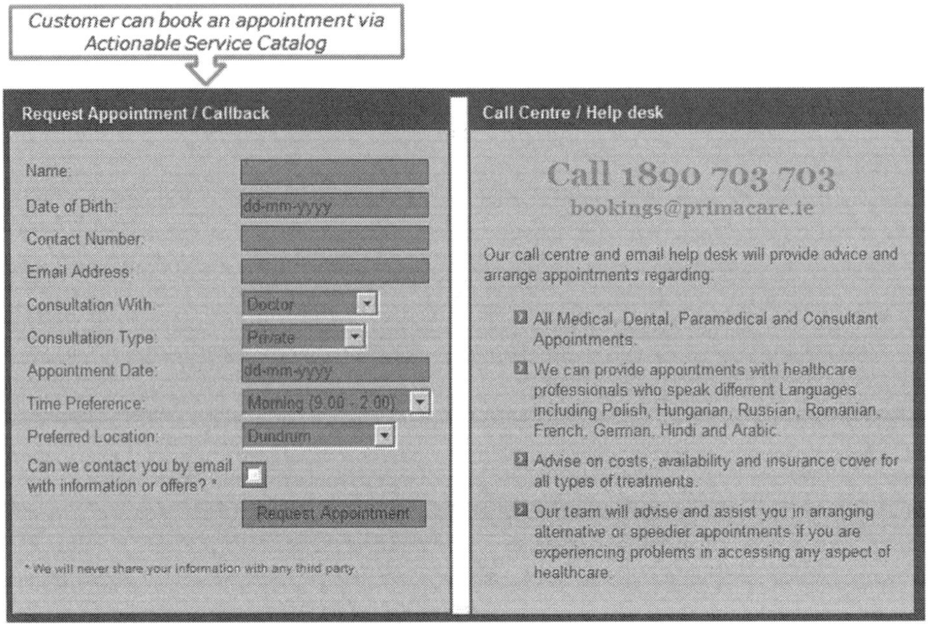

Customer can book an appointment via
Actionable Service Catalog

Request Appointment / Callback

Name:

Date of Birth: dd-mm-yyyy

Contact Number:

Email Address:

Consultation With: Doctor

Consultation Type: Private

Appointment Date: dd-mm-yyyy

Time Preference: Morning (9.00 - 2.00)

Preferred Location: Dundrum

Can we contact you by email
with information or offers? *

Request Appointment

* We will never share your information with any third party

Call Centre / Help desk

Call 1890 703 703
bookings@primacare.ie

Our call centre and email help desk will provide advice and
arrange appointments regarding:

- All Medical, Dental, Paramedical and Consultant
  Appointments.

- We can provide appointments with healthcare
  professionals who speak different Languages
  including Polish, Hungarian, Russian, Romanian,
  French, German, Hindi and Arabic.

- Advise on costs, availability and insurance cover for
  all types of treatments.

- Our team will advise and assist you in arranging
  alternative or speedier appointments if you are
  experiencing problems in accessing any aspect of
  healthcare.

Figure B.3 Example of booking service (Source www.primacare.ie)

Appendix C. Acronyms

API	–	Application Programming Interface (API)
BOK	–	Body of Knowledge
CI	–	Configuration Item
CIO	–	Chief Information Officer
COBIT	–	Control Objectives for Information and Related Technology
CMDB	–	Configuration Management Database
CMS	–	Configuration Management System
CSI	–	Continual Service Improvement
DSL	–	Definitive Software Library
ERP	–	Enterprise Resource Planning
ISO	–	International Organization for Standardization
ITIL	–	Information Technology Infrastructure Library
itSMF	–	IT Service Management Forum
KPI	–	Key Performance Indicator
MOF	–	Microsoft Operations Framework
OGC	–	Office of Government Commerce
OLA	–	Operational Level Agreement
QoS	–	Quality of Service
RFC	–	Request for Change
ROI	–	Return on Investment
SACM	–	Service Asset & Configuration Management
SCD	–	Supplier and Contracts Database
SLA	–	Service Level Agreement
SLR	–	Service Lever Requirement
SLT	–	Service Level Targets
SPACL	–	Service Portfolio and Catalog Language
SPO	–	Service Provider Organization
SPOC	–	Single Point of Contact
UC	–	Underpinning Contract
USMBOK	–	The Universal Service Management Body of Knowledge
VOI	–	Value on Investment

Appendix D. Frameworks

The following table provides a brief description of the frameworks referenced throughout this book and includes the links to their main websites where further information can be found.

Name	Type	Description[25]	More Information
ITIL®	Good practice	Information Technology Infrastructure Library (ITIL®) is the most widely accepted approach to IT service management in the world. ITIL provides a cohesive set of good practice, drawn from the public and private sectors internationally.	http://www.best-management-practice.com/
CobiT®	Framework	Control Objectives for Information and Related Technology (CobiT) is an IT governance framework and supporting toolset that allows managers to bridge the gap between control requirements, technical issues and business risks. CobiT enables clear policy development and good practice for IT control throughout organizations. CobiT emphasizes regulatory compliance, helps organizations to increase the value attained from IT, enables alignment and simplifies implementation of the CobiT framework.	www.isaca.org/cobit/
MOF	Framework	Microsoft® Operations Framework (MOF) 4.0 delivers practical guidance for everyday IT practices and activities, helping users establish and implement reliable, cost-effective IT services.	http://www.microsoft.com/mof
ISO/IEC 20000-1:2005	Standard	Defines the requirements for a service provider to deliver quality managed services.	http://www.iso.org/iso/catalogue_detail?csnumber=41332
USMBOK™	Body of Knowledge	The Universal Service Management Body of Knowledge (USMBOK) is derived from published literature and the accumulated experiences of practitioners in the service management profession. It continues to evolve as the profession evolves, through open dialog and representation.	http://www.usmbok.org/
ISM™	Toolkit	Integrated Service Management (ISM) is a total solution that is delivered out-of-the-box, providing access to a complete management portal and all the resources needed to implement a process-based approach. These resources are delivered as a standard part of the ISM Portal.	http://www.ismportal.nl/en

Table D.1 IT service management frameworks

---

23 All descriptions have been taken from the respective websites.

Appendix E. Service level agreement

The following table lists the most common content that can, and should be, included in an SLA. This content provided in table E.1 can be easily incorporated into any organizations own documentation templates.

Description	Details
Cover page	Set headers and footers, page and version control numbering.
Distribution list	Is generally a table. Record of who should be included on the distribution of the SLA. Include as columns: name, department and email address.
Document version control	Is generally a table. Record brief description of modifications and changes to the SLA. Include as columns: name, role and description of change.
Version	Version of the document, for example version 1.21. Use major revision & minor revision numbering. Ensure version numbering is updated after major/minor changes.
Authorization details	Is generally a table. Record who should be included as the authorizers of the SLA. The people listed here will be required to authorize the first official version of the SLA and also any major updates. Include as columns: name, role, date each person approved.
Author details	Add the name of the author(s).
Table of contents	Generate a table of contents.
Scope of document	Define the scope of the SLA clearly. What is in-scope and what is out- of scope.
Objectives of document	Define the objectives of the SLA. The objective of the SLA document is to record the details of the service being provided and in particular record the level of service that will be provided.
Commencement date	Record the date that the SLA comes into effect.
Duration of agreement	Record the term that the SLA will be in effect for and document the end/termination date.
Review date	The SLA should be under document review cycle to ensure that it remains valid. Requirements may change during the lifetime that the SLA is in existence and may need to be updated within the SLA. At the very least it is good practice to review important documentation periodically.
Review cycle	Specify the frequency that the SLA will be reviewed, for example yearly.
Description of service	Document a description of the service. The description may make reference to the standard service and any extended service offerings that may exist.

Description	Details
Agreed service hours	Detail the hours that the service will be provided. Include any exceptions, weekends, public holidays, company days, et cetera. Example: The service will be provided and supported during normal service hours. Normal service hours are Monday to Sunday 9.00hrs to 21.00hrs including public holidays.
Service availability & service targets	Detail the agreed availability of the service. As the SLA is for an agreed "business or customer" service, availability must not just be focused on the availability of the IT services. Example: The service will be available to users/customers as per the agreed service hours. Due to the fact that there is no web service redundancy, the customer website that forms part of this service offering will have an agreed availability target of 98% uptime during the *agreed service hours*.
Priority matrix	Applicable in some instances. Example: In the case of a service desk this would consist of a table that shows priorities based on impact & urgency. Other matrix possibilities exist.
Support details & hours	Include specific details regarding: • who supports the service and at what level • support hour times - Note: these should match with the agreed service hours to ensure quality of service. However this is not always the case. Note any exceptions here. • how to contact the relevant support group. In some cases this is via a SPOC (single point of contact); service desk.
Maintenance windows	This records an agreed window of time when unplanned or unscheduled interruptions can take place to the service. Maintenance windows should be planned during times where there is little or no demand for the service, for example out of hours and over weekends. Change management can help to establish maintenance windows and enforce their use.
Scheduled maintenance	This should reference any scheduled or planned maintenance around the service as a whole. Specific references may be made to IT systems and services. Example: Once every three months the customer website will be taken off line during non service hours in order to apply the latest application and security patches. This activity will be under strict change management control.
Service charging	If charging is to be applied to the service it should be stated clearly and in enough detail that avoids any possible misinterpretation at a later date. Details of how and when potential service credits or penalties can and should be applied need to be stated in clear terms.
Exceptions	Note any exceptions that apply to the service.

Description	Details
Performance targets	This section records the agreed targets that will be used to measure the performance of the service. Targets should be focused on demonstrating required outcomes and will generally measure and report outputs. Targets can also be referred to as service level targets or SLT's. In practice, SLT's may, in error, be perceived solely as the actual service level agreement.
Service reporting	Include details about: • the types of report that will be provided • the schedule for completing and sending reports • how to deal with ad-hoc report requests • agreed service report templates may be included in or referenced from an appendix
Escalation management	Detail the procedure for handling escalations. Escalations should be prioritized and dealt with accordingly depending on how serious the escalation. Include details on how to define the priority of an escalation.
Complaints procedure	Provide details on the agreed manner for handling complaints in relation to the service. Complaints may require an escalation.
Changes to service	Document the change management procedures, or reference existing procedures, that are to be used to effect any changes to the service that are not considered to be within the normal operating parameters of the service.
Service reviews	Provide details of the review cycle for the actual service (not the SLA document). When - The schedule of when the reviews will take place. Who - The people that are to be involved in the reviews. What - Scope of the review. Why - Objectives of the review. How - Roles & responsibilities of people involved.
Sign-off from signatories	Record the signatures of the key people that are required to sign the SLA. Ensure to scan the signatures page and append it to the soft copy of the SLA.
Glossary of terms	Provide an explanation of terms in the document.
Appendices	Include any additional information as required e.g. service report templates.

Table E.1 Content that should be included in an SLA

Sources

Literature
- Brooks, Peter. *Metrics for IT Service Management* (2006). Zaltbommel: Van Haren Publishing.
- Bon, J. van, et al (Ed.). *Foundations of IT Service management based on ITIL V3* (2008). Zaltbommel: Van Haren Publishing 2008.
- Bon, J. van, et al (Ed.). *ISO/IEC 20000 An Introduction* (2008). Zaltbommel: Van Haren Publishing.
- Bon, J. van, et al (Ed.). *IT Service Management Global Best Practices*, Volume 1 (2008). Zaltbommel: Van Haren Publishing.
- Bon, J. van, et al (Ed.). *World Class IT Service Management Guide* (2000). The Hague: ten Hagen & Stam Publishers.
- OGC. *ITIL: Continual Service Improvement* (2007). London: TSO.
- OGC. *ITIL: Service Delivery* (2001). London: TSO.
- OGC. *ITIL: Service Design* (2007). London: TSO.
- OGC. *ITIL: Service Operation* (2007). London: TSO.
- OGC. *ITIL: Service Strategy* (2007). London: TSO.
- OGC. *ITIL: Service Transition* (2007). London: TSO.
- Sottini, Maxime. *IT Financial Management* (2009).Zaltbommel: Van Haren Publishing.
- Tricker, R. *ISO 9001:2000 The Quality Management Process* (2006). Van Haren Publishing.

Web
- Frequently Asked Questions UNSPC.
  http://www.unspsc.org/FAQs.asp#whyclassify, UNSPC 2009.
- ITIL Glossary.
  http://www.best-management-practice.com/gempdf/ITILV3_Glossary_English_v1_2007.pdf
- Larry English quote.
  http://www.dmreview.com/issues/20010201/3009-1.html
- MOF.
  http://technet.microsoft.com/en-us/library/cc506049.aspx
- Primacare example.
  http://www.primacare.ie/
- Some definitions.
  http://en.wikipedia.org/
- Service Catalog.
  http://www.apmgroup.co.uk/ServiceCatalogue/ServiceCatalogue.asp, APM Group 2009.
- Service Portfolio and Catalog Language - Public review site for SPACL documents.
  http://www.spacl.info/, SPACL 2009.
- The ITIL Credit Profiler System.
  http://www.itil-officialsite.com/itilservices/v1/map.asp, APM Group 2009.
- USMBOK question reference.
  http://www.sm101-support.com/kb_article.php?ref=1521-UMZI-4400

Index

Made in the USA
Lexington, KY
13 May 2013